THE REFERENCE SHELF (*Continued*)

Volume 22

No. 3. Representative American Speeches: 1949-1950. A. C. Baird. $1.75.

Volume 21

No. 2. Representative American Speeches: 1948-1949. A. C. Baird. $1.75.

Volume 20

No.
5. Federal World Government. J. E. Johnsen. $1.50.

No.
6. Federal Information Controls in Peacetime. R. E. Summers. $1.50.

Volume 19

No. 3. Free Medical Care. C. A. Peters. $1.25.

Volume 18

No.
3. Representative American Speeches: 1944-1945. A. C. Baird. $1.25.
5. Anatomy of Racial Intolerance. G. B. de Huszar. $1.25.

No.
6. Palestine: Jewish Homeland? J. E. Johnsen. $1.25.

Volume 17

No. 4. Representative American Speeches: 1943-1944. A. C. Baird. $1.25.

Volume 16

No.
1. Representative American Speeches: 1941-1942. A. C. Baird. $1.25.

No.
6. Representative American Speeches: 1942-1943. A. C. Baird. $1.25.

Volume 15

No.
1. Representative American Speeches: 1940-1941. A. C. Baird. $1.25.
2. Universal Military Service. R. E. Summers and H. B. Summers. $1.25.
3. Federal Regulation of Labor Unions. J. V. Garland. $1.25.

No.
7. The Closed Shop. J. E. Johnsen. $1.25.

9. Permanent Price Control Policy. J. E. Johnsen. $1.25.

10. A Federal Sales Tax. E. R. Nichols. $1.25.

THE REFERENCE SHELF

Vol. 27   No. 6

U. S. POLICY
IN ASIA

Edited by
WILLIAM W. WADE

THE H. W. WILSON COMPANY
NEW YORK   1955

15136

PREFACE

Until World War II we Americans tended to argue about United States policy toward Europe, while we took policy in the Far East more or less for granted. Europe was properly regarded as the more important center of world power, Asia as a backwater. Our Far Eastern policy, in addition to its secondary role, was a subject on which there was broad national agreement. Few voices dissented from our main interests of safeguarding our strategic position in the Pacific, in keeping an open door for trade and in carrying out missionary, educational, and other philanthropic activities. Most of us knew little about only a few of Asia's many lands. We were friendly well-wishers of turbulent China. As war came closer, we were suspicious of Japan's militarism. We were sympathetic to India's quest for independence, and we were sincere in our intention of granting sovereignty to our own colonial outpost, the Philippines. The rest of Asia we knew less well. We were aware only dimly, if at all, of the different peoples, problems and ways of life that stretched from the Khyber Pass to the Celebes Sea.

Today the picture is sharply different. We have learned—and are learning—of many of Asia's complexities. Some of the lessons have been painful. We recognize that Asian events can be directly related to our own well-being; we have buried our dead in the Korean hills. As a result, our Far Eastern policy has become one of the most controversial subjects on our political scene. We argue strenuously among ourselves about the proper course of action our government should take. And at times, we argue even more heatedly about the past—about how we got to where we now are in our relations with Asia.

Looking back we can see that the Japanese attack on Pearl Harbor was only the starting point for a chain of events that accelerated Asian history. The war in the Far East, like wars everywhere, not only changed the map, it changed life in the villages as well. The war's outcome stripped Japan of Korea and

Formosa; through the Yalta agreement it gave the Soviet Union a privileged position in Manchuria. It spurred Asian nationalism, soon resulting in a whole array of newly independent states —India, Pakistan, Ceylon, Burma, the Philippines and Indonesia. And it set the stage for the most portentous event of all, the Chinese civil war.

The fall of China's mainland to communism in 1949 was a disastrous blow to American interests and aspirations in Asia. Not only did it add China's millions to Communist ranks, but it swiftly threatened to spill over on all sides. It was followed by Communist aggression in Korea, bald Chinese intervention after United Nations troops had repelled the aggressors and then a bitter, stalemated war ending in an uneasy truce in 1953. After Korea, France's costly and ill-fated struggle to suppress the Communist-led Vietminh in Indo-China became the next international crisis. And when that was settled at Geneva in 1954 by conceding part of the country to the Vietminh, China's Communists threatened once more to attempt an assault on Formosa, refuge of Chiang Kai-shek's Nationalists.

With this series of crises behind us, it is no wonder that we debate Far Eastern policy with fervor, that we are assailed by doubts, and that we offer conflicting views on the right way to achieve our aims in Asia. This volume contains a few of the facts, ideas and opinions that are currently going into this debate. The book does not dwell heavily on the past; it is designed to guide discussion of the present and the future. It is in part a survey of free Asia and in part a collection of varied views on how the United States can help maintain that freedom, give it strength, and make it grow.

Acknowledgment is gratefully given to the many authors and publishers who have courteously granted permission to reprint copyrighted material.

WILLIAM W. WADE

August 1955

CONTENTS

V. THE PROBLEM OF CHINA

THE ARC OF FREE ASIA: POPULATION 771 MILLION

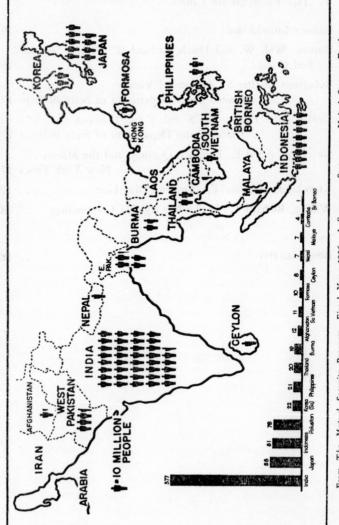

From *The Mutual Security Program, Fiscal Year 1956, A Summary Statement.* United States. Foreign Operations Administration. Washington 25, D.C. May 1955. p43.

I. THE CHALLENGE WE FACE

EDITOR'S INTRODUCTION

Since the end of the Korean war, the United States has been attempting to build defenses in Asia that will withstand Communist assaults whether they come in the form of further military aggression, subversion and guerrilla warfare or, under the guise of peace, as economic and political competition.

These efforts failed to prevent the 1954 Geneva settlement of France's lengthy war in Indo-China, an agreement that had serious shortcomings in American eyes.

Washington's policy-makers, have made headway elsewhere, but it is still too early to determine whether they will be successful in achieving the strength, stability, and peace we seek in Asia. Throughout 1955 there has been the continued Chinese Communist threat of renewed hostilities in the Formosa Straits and a possible attack on the island stronghold of the Republic of China, the Chinese government which we continue to recognize and which still holds China's seat in the United Nations. Other unsolved issues heighten tension between the United States and Red China, including Peiping's continued imprisonment of American civilians.

There have been two important developments in United States efforts to deal with the challenges of Asia. One has been the negotiation of new treaties; the other the renewal and broadening of our foreign aid program in the Far East.

The Southeast Asia Treaty Organization—SEATO—is an attempt to repeat the success of the North Atlantic Treaty Organization in the Pacific. The SEATO treaty, signed in September 1954, was designed to provide the "united action" that might help prevent another Indo-China. Its drawback was that it failed to win the support of important Asian nations including India, Indonesia and Burma.

At the same time, American policy-makers were increasingly concerned with the economic challenge—with the fact that China's industrial and agricultural development under totalitarianism might outstrip development under democratic methods in India and other nations. The West, it was recognized, must not only continue to outperform the Communists but must also help underdeveloped countries to do the same. Thus, the Eisenhower Administration sought an increased aid program for Asia on a long-range basis even as it carried out the termination, fixed by Congress, of the Foreign Operations Administration—successor to the Economic Cooperation Administration and the Mutual Security Agency. The President prevailed upon Congress to appropriate substantial sums for both military and economic assistance in free Asia in the 1956 fiscal year, and the FOA's functions were taken over by a new International Cooperation Administration, an adjunct of the State Department.

Meanwhile, Asia itself was speaking up. Twenty-nine Asian and African nations sent their prime ministers and other officials to a meeting at Bandung, Indonesia, in April 1955. The meeting was called by the so-called Colombo powers—India, Ceylon, Pakistan, Indonesia and Burma—which had themselves held two conferences in 1954 to exchange views on world affairs. Bandung, economics and the threat of Communist aggression were thus all part of the challenge faced by the United States in Asia. The following articles summarize these problems in brief form, as seen by administrators of our economic aid program, by a State Department spokesman and by several journalists well-acquainted with Asia.

REAPPRAISING ASIAN POLICY [1]

Washington has begun to awaken uncomfortably . . . to the political reality of neutralist Free Asia [as the result of the Afro-Asian conference at Bandung, Indonesia, in April 1955].

[1] From "U.S. Now Reappraising Its Policies Toward Free Asia," news story by Dana Adams Schmidt, New York *Times* Washington correspondent. New York *Times.* p E4. May 8, 1955. Reprinted by permission.

Asia and Asian sentiments are hardly new. What is new is that at Bandung, the Asians expressed themselves for the first time in their own forum, in a babel of voices critical of both the political East and the political West.

Washington was surprised that the conference showed that this country has more, and more vigorous friends in Asia than it realized, and impressed by indications that the solid show of Asian opposition to aggressive expansionism induced the Chinese Communist Chou En-lai to offer to talk over the Formosa crisis directly with the United States.

And Washington appears also to have taken serious note of the lack of sympathy for Chiang Kai-shek and his cause, even among some of the United States' most trusted Allies, of the cold disapproval of talk about defending Quemoy and Matsu, and of the general Asian dismay when the United States seemed to be stalling on Chou's offer to talk.

Free Asia emerged from that conference as a political force to be reckoned with. In consequence, policy-making officials here have been asking a great many questions. They are most concerned with the area foreign aid director Harold Stassen dubbed "The Arc of Free Asia." Extending around the periphery of Communist China, from Afghanistan and Pakistan to Korea and Japan, it is the area most immediately menaced by Communist infiltration and expansionism.

Who lives in this area? What are their problems? How can they be influenced? These are the basic questions.

Here are some of the answers:

In this area live 771 million people—one third of the human race, in fifteen countries—Afghanistan, Thailand, the Philippines, Japan, the Republic of China (Formosa), India, Nepal, Pakistan, Ceylon, Burma, South Vietnam, Cambodia, Laos, Indonesia and South Korea. . . . All but a few of these countries have attained independence only since World War II.

With the exception of Japan, which is highly industrialized and highly literate and enjoys relatively high standards of health and living, these fifteen countries share many problems that shape their political attitudes.

Especially in the new states, nationalism is intense and goes hand in hand with resentment of Western colonialism and general suspicion of the white man. All are immensely ambitious to industrialize and raise their standards of living. They see Communist China making giant strides in this direction by ruthless totalitarian means, and they are impressed and respectful—the more so because China is an Asian nation.

Western ideas of democracy are at a disadvantage in many of these countries, firstly, because they are represented mainly by white men; secondly, because their operation is slow and complex; thirdly, because the political and material standards of the West seem unattainable.

Rightly or wrongly, these Asians blame their former Western rulers for the lack of development of local industry and regional trade, and their lopsided dependence on raw materials exports to uncertain Western markets—jute, cotton, tin, rubber, copra, kapok, etc.

The average annual per capita income in the whole area is about $100. India's is only $57, Indonesia's $25. Furthermore, the swift expansion of population in stagnant economies has actually lowered standards of living in many of the countries since prewar days.

The countries planning their own industrialization shortsightedly see in Japan only a competitor. She must fight hard and long to reestablish old trade relations and gain new ones in Asia.

Encountering stiff sales resistance throughout the free world, uncertain how long they can count on United States military expenditures to cover their trade deficit, the Japanese are tempted to deal with Communist China and the Soviet Union. Although the government is pledged to cooperation with the United States, popular anti-Americanism is rising.

Illiteracy and disease are terrible burdens. The Philippines and Formosa are 65 per cent literate, Indonesia 55 per cent, India 20 per cent, Pakistan 14 per cent. Life expectancy is 49 years in Thailand, 32 in Indonesia and India, 27 in Pakistan. In Indo-China there is only one physician per 59,000 persons.

The key countries in the area, from many points of view, are Japan, India, and Indonesia, which lie roughly at the corners of a triangle.

Japan, with a population of 80 millions, is the only thoroughly industrialized country. Not only must she export to the others to live; she could serve as their workshop, providing them with tools for their own development, if the others would only accept her services.

But wartime hatreds have proven long-lasting in Asia. What Japan should and can pay in reparations has not yet been settled.

The United States looks to Japan as its most essential ally in the Far East. But as her government, under the pressure of genuine antimilitarist sentiment combined with left wing opposition, systematically shirks the burdens of rearmament, doubts about this ally's value and reliability have arisen.

Indonesia, whose population is 81 millions, is the region's great purveyor of raw materials—rubber, oil, and tin. These resources make her both an invaluable source of supply to the United States and potentially the richest country in the region. But since they drove out the Dutch the Indonesians have retrogressed economically amidst the uncertainties and preoccupations of internal dissension.

Various dissident groups in West and Central Java, Northern Sumatra and the Celebes keep Indonesia from settling down to business. Although a Communist insurrection was suppressed in 1948 the Communists have been allowed to continue operations in the guise of supporters of the coalition government. They are so influential and the government is so weak that neutralism becomes the only possible policy.

India, with 360 million rapidly multiplying inhabitants, is by far the most populous country, and the greatest market. Exploiting her varied and considerable resources, India is now in the fourth year of a five-year development plan. She has made steady progress, especially in food production. But the industrial side lags. She still has 20 million unemployed. Half the rural population is idle except in the growing season. Chances of attaining the aim of doubling the per capita national income by 1977 are not very good.

Yet India carries a heavy military burden—partly, no doubt, to offset Pakistan in the Kashmir and water disputes, but also because neutralist Premier Nehru—so it is reported by diplomats who know him personally—knows that the real menace to his country is Communist China.

Meanwhile all of Asia watches the progress of neutralist but democratic India, comparing her development with that of Communist China, and drawing conclusions.

Among these three great countries, Japan, Indonesia and India, and among the others in between, lively trade could obviously be developed. Unfortunately regional trade is only just beginning, with United States encouragement, to get the attention it merits.

THE VULNERABILITY OF ASIA [2]

The free world is threatened by the most dangerous aggressive power in human history. In combination, the Soviet Union and Communist China dominate the largest area and population ever controlled by a single center of power. They maintain the largest collection of men under arms ever assembled in peacetime. They possess nuclear weapons and are steadily increasing their nuclear capabilities. They possess great quantities of basic natural resources. Uninhibited by moral or humanitarian considerations, the Soviet-Chinese leaders have imposed on the areas they control a massive system of slavery under which all human and material resources are marshalled in pursuit of the expansion of Communist power. These leaders have vowed that their system will eventually dominate the entire world.

The menace of Soviet-Chinese communism is not so much its politico-economic *theory*, as its *practice* of using force, and

[2] From *The Mutual Security Program, Fiscal Year 1956, A Summary Statement.* Foreign Operations Administration. Washington, D.C. May 1955. p5-6, 43-7.

threats of force, to attain its stated goal of world domination and control. For example: . . .

In the Far East, following World War II, Communist-inspired armed bands engaged in acts of insurrection in the Philippines, in Malaya, in Burma and in Indonesia.

In 1949, Chinese Communist armies forced the mainland of China to become a Communist state.

In 1950 Communist armies from North Korea crossed over the 38th parallel and invaded the Republic of Korea. The North Korean Communists were subsequently abetted in their aggressive actions by about 1.5 million Chinese Communist "volunteers."

In 1951 Chinese Communists acquired, through threats of force, control over Tibet.

In 1954 Communist-led forces in Indo-China succeeded in gaining control of north Vietnam.

Coupled with the threat and use of armed force international communism has developed and used other techniques to weaken nations outside the Soviet-Chinese bloc and to build up the power of the bloc. The Communists have proved themselves adept at the insidious art of subversion from the inside. Espionage and infiltration of institutions—government agencies, trade unions, communications media—propaganda in massive amounts, attempts to use trade, and offers of trade, for military and political purposes—all of these, in the past ten years, have become well-recognized tactics. The progressive increase in these tactics of nonmilitary penetration is visible in the greatly increased participation of the Soviet Union in trade fairs in many free countries of the world; in offers of trade agreements, of technical assistance, and of aid in economic development.

Through all these means, between 1945 and 1950, aggressive communism took over fourteen nations in Europe and Asia, covering over five million square miles and including more than 700 million people. . . .

The arc of free Asia extends from the Middle East through South and Southeast Asia to Japan and Korea on the East. Its land area is 3.7 million square miles—9 per cent of the free world. Its population is about 770 million persons, almost one half of the free world. Yet these great masses live on only 11 per cent of the free world's output of goods and services.

This group of countries is a most important area—and a most vulnerable one. Its first importance is of course because of its people—its tremendous number of people who are now free, and hopeful of remaining so. It is also an area of great military-strategic significance, lying as it does in a great arc of freedom around the center of Communist power in Asia. This region includes the new states of Southeast Asia which are particularly accessible to Communist expansion, either by overt aggression or by internal subversion. It includes also the island chain which constitutes our defense line in the Pacific, and the mainland and islands which lie athwart free world air and sea communications, commercial and defensive, between the Pacific, South Asia and Europe.

It is in the interests of the United States that these free nations remain free and that responsible governments be able to maintain themselves against forces of subversion and fragmentation.

It is in our interest to assist the nations of South Asia, even though in some cases their foreign policies may not coincide with ours, if it is their firm policy to remain free. The South Asian governments value their recently acquired independence and substantial elements in all these countries realize the threat to progress and freedom which the Communist parties in the area constitute. In most of these countries the fight being waged against these parties is vigorous and unrelenting. These free nations, like ourselves, are dedicated to peace, stability and security. They need assistance in this critical period while attempting, within a democratic framework, to achieve the military strength and the economic progress required to help assure their political independence.

The psychological impact of further dramatic Communist successes in South and Southeast Asia would be particularly serious in other areas of Asia and the Near East which are striving to attain economic advancement and political stability under democratic institutions. The claim of Communist China to possess and be practicing the only effective formula for rapidly improving the material well-being of underdeveloped and densely populated countries, would be greatly strengthened. Undesirable consequences to political systems in other free nations might be expected to follow.

These nations are also important to us economically. They are sources of vital raw materials required by Western world defense and civilian goods industries; they furnish important markets for some of the products of our highly industrialized economy though, despite their vast population, with their present low incomes, they purchase only 10 to 12 per cent of our exports; and they make an important contribution to a well balanced distribution of world trade and investment. In respect to sources of raw materials, over 90 per cent of the free world rubber, tea and jute and over 85 per cent of its rice comes from South and Southeast Asia. Tin, mica, manganese, chrome and tungsten are other strategic items on which our dependence is very substantial. In addition, Japan relies on Southeast Asia for its oil, bauxite and iron ore supplies as well as for large amounts of food and textile raw materials. To Japan, trade with this area is one possible alternative to trade with Communist China. Thirty-three per cent of her exports now go to Southeast Asia as compared with 16 per cent before the war. In return for the strategic and other materials furnished to the United States and Japan, the area imports large quantities of industrial equipment and consumer goods from these countries and from Western Europe.

At present the military forces of Communist aggression have been checked in the Far East. Internal subversion remains a serious threat, particularly in free Vietnam. It is a smoldering menace in Malaya, Indonesia and to a lesser extent in the Philippines. In countries in South Asia more remote from the threat of an armed Communist offensive, strenuous efforts are being made by the Soviet bloc to cultivate and intensify anti-Western, and particularly anti-American, sentiments. This offensive is taking the form, among others, of propaganda disseminated within the countries by disaffected groups such as unemployed intellectuals. Realizing their appeal, and the subversive use that can be made of them, Russia has increased sharply her proffers of technical assistance, and even capital equipment, with the outwardly expressed purpose of contributing to economic development programs. Russia has started a pattern of significant economic penetration through a series of economic development projects and with technicians from the Iron Curtain countries. Offers through the Economic Commission for Asia and the Far East (ECAFE) of all-expenses-paid "observation" trips to Russia, Communist Chinese programs of "education" for overseas Chinese, and offers of technical assistance in economic planning in India are recent examples. Russia has made a particularly significant offer of a million-ton steel mill to India. The steel mill would not be a gift to India, but tentative agreement has been reached providing for its financing on a long term, low interest loan basis. Russian capital and technicians are involved in a number of major projects in Afghanistan. Indonesia was offered a $16 million loan to restore sugar mills. A point strongly emphasized in Soviet propaganda surrounding these projects is the claim that Western countries such as the United Kingdom and the United States do not want heavy industry in under-developed countries.

The belief is widely held in Asia that Red China, by the redistribution of existing property and claims of stepping up the rate of capital formation, is in the vanguard of economic development. At the same time, most Asian leaders now realize that the tyranny, anti-religious ideology and police state methods of Peking are some of the prices paid for such purported advancement under communism. Thus, we find in important Asian countries a reaction to communism which takes the form of strengthening measures against subversive influences within, even while they have a mixture of admiration and fear for alleged Communist accomplishments outside their borders.

In the Republic of Korea and Vietnam, countries but recently wracked by a Communist military onslaught, priority attention must be paid to reconstruction, as well as economic development. At the same time, defense forces must be built up and maintained to help cope with a possible renewed attack.

Formosa a special problem has arisen from the aggressive
posture of Red China. The Manila-pact powers, Pakistan,
Thailand and the Philippines are steadfast in their determination
to increase their military contributions to Asian security even
while carrying forward programs related to the economic and
anti-subversion provisions of that treaty.

A STATE DEPARTMENT VIEW [3]

Before attempting to analyze the main elements in our
Asian policy, I should like to emphasize . . . that it is a fundamental mistake to think of Asia as an entity. This vast area
comprehends a sweeping arc from the maritime provinces of
Russia down through Japan and China, through the Southeast
Asian Peninsula and its adjacent islands, on through Ceylon,
Pakistan, and India and up through the Middle East. Asia
represents not a unity but an enormous diversity of ethnic
origins, cultures, religious beliefs, and traditions. Migrations
have taken place in Asia since the dawn of time, so that the
presence of minority groups is quite common. In contrast to
Japan and Korea, where the national languages alone are spoken
and the people are homogeneous, there are nations like India
where a dozen major languages and scores of local dialects are
spoken. Economies vary widely from the advanced industrial
and trading complex of Japan to the relatively simple agricultural economies which are found in many of the other Asian
countries. The political attitudes of the Asian nations are also
characterized not by uniformity but by diversity and even by
deep-seated conflict on some issues. Certain of the nations must
be restrained from incendiary aggressive actions. Others are so
determined to pursue an independent neutral course that they
refuse to undertake what we regard as minimum defensive
measures. Among the free nations of the area there is not even
a consistent pattern of diplomatic recognition. This is par-

[3] From "Our Policies in Asia," address by Robert D. Murphy, Deputy Under
Secretary of State, before the World Affairs Forum of the Foreign Policy Association of Pittsburgh, May 5, 1955. *United States Department of State Bulletin.*
32:835-40. May 23, 1955.

ticularly true on the question of recognition as between Communist China and the government of the Republic of China on Formosa.

This lack of homogeneity in Asia, this pervasive diversity, is not always a pleasant fact to deal with, but it is a fact which we must take fully into account in the process of policy formulation. Fundamentally, of course, our policy in Asia, as elsewhere in the world, is designed to protect and promote the security and welfare of the American people. We do that in Asia primarily by assisting the friendly nations there to build up their strength so that their independence can be preserved against all efforts to destroy it. However, from a practical standpoint, our approach in Asia takes the form of a number of policies, each carefully cut to the measure of the specific situation we face. In this sense, our "Asian policy" is really a combination of many policies formulated in terms of realistic situations but designed to encourage national independence, economic improvement, friendly cooperation with the United States, and peace.

Having stressed the diversity of the Asian scene, let me now further emphasize it by offering you a contradiction in the form of a single factor which is universal to the area. This factor is nationalism, a force which has been fundamental in shaping the course of events throughout the length and breadth of Asia in our time. Nationalistic sensitivities are an important factor in our dealings with all of the Asian nations, even those which are most friendly with us. Nationalism played a pivotal role in the negotiation of our security agreement with Japan, for that agreement called for the stationing of United States forces on the soil of a proud and sensitive people. Nationalism figures in the determination of the Korean people to unify their peninsula and in the magnificent performance of the South Koreans when their homeland was invaded from the north. In a different way, nationalism is a factor in the hesitancy of certain of the Asian nations to accept United States aid. It is a basic motivation of the friendly Vietnamese government of Premier Diem. It even accounts in part for the rise of Ho Chi

Minh in his guise as the liberator of Vietnam. It animates the determined neutrality of India.

To these powerful nationalistic motivations is linked a sometimes extreme anticolonialism. This is a factor which the Communists have exploited with cunning skill. Yet it is an attitude—a neurosis, if you will—with which the United States of America perhaps more than any other of the great nations of the world can wholeheartedly sympathize. For it was not so very long ago in terms of history that we took up arms to free ourselves from tyranny. . . .

Our tradition of opposition to absolutism and empire has created strong bonds with many Asian peoples. And our deeds have shown that we were in earnest. We threw in our lot against the carving up of China by the European monarchies. We convinced the Filipinos that the main objective of the American administration was their independence. We raised our voice against the abuses of the prewar regimes in Asia and refused to countenance the extension of Japan's imperial rule over China in the 1930's. We freely renounced our extraterritorial privileges in China, and we made the liberation of Korea a World War II objective.

The record, over a long period, is a consistent one. By 1945, many of the Asian nations, emerging at last from the long twilight of colonialism, looked to us for leadership and for guidance. In the decade that has passed since then, our relations with Asia have become vastly more complicated, in part because they have become more extensive and more intimate. Before World War II we had official relations with six Asian nations. Now we have relations with twenty-six. Our economic and technical aid programs, our military aid programs, our joint membership in international bodies like the United Nations and its subsidiaries, our interlocking commercial interests—all these have brought us into much closer contact with the peoples of Asia with each succeeding year.

To some Asians our motives remain suspect, but there are reasons to believe that the masses of Asia respect us. In many ways the Bandung conference [in April 1955], at which twenty-nine Asian and African nations met for the first time to discuss matters of mutual interest and plans for mutual progress, was a heartening affirmation of that confidence. I am sure you are all familiar with the outspoken espousals of the free world cause and the outright condemnations of communism which were expressed at Bandung by the astute statements of the leaders of such countries as Iran, Iraq, Pakistan, Turkey, Ceylon, Thailand, and the Philippines. Those vigorous speeches were obviously sincere manifestations of nationalism and of a determination to defend the principles of independence and freedom. They were fully reported by the free press and warmly received throughout the free world. Significantly, the Communist world did not repeat them by press and radio to its enslaved peoples.

There is no doubt that those speeches were effective, for the final communiqué of the conference, while still reflecting the vestigial fears of Western imperialism, stated that the conference, had agreed "in declaring that colonialism in all its manifestations is an evil which should speedily be brought to an end." Thus the conference condemned the new colonialism of communism as well as the outmoded nineteenth-century variety. The communiqué also recognized the principle of "respect for the right of each nation to defend itself singly or collectively in conformity with the Charter of the United Nations." This was an endorsement of the collective security principle which is the foundation for so much of our effort in Asia and elsewhere to deal with the problem of aggression.

Here is progress indeed. And there is one more quotation from this interesting final communiqué worth mentioning—a credit to the United States under the heading entitled "Economic Cooperation" saying:

It was further recognized that assistance being received by certain participating countries from outside the region through international or under bilateral arrangements had made a valuable contribution to the implementation of their development programs.

This was a recognition by the participants that foreign economic aid programs, such as those of the United States, are a welcome and constructive kind of international activity.

The significance of those resolutions is even greater when you consider that they were approved unanimously by the conference. I think that they demonstrate how close our own policies are to the spirit which prevailed at Bandung. As I have pointed out, ever since the swaddling days of our own liberty, America has been deeply unsympathetic to colonialism. The encouragement of nationalist aspirations is simply the other side of the same coin, and this has been our consistent policy in Asia as elsewhere in the world.

The latest example of such encouragement has been our consistent support of the independence of the government of free Vietnam at a time of very great stress and strain in that outpost of freedom. With our ally, France, we are making every effort to help the government of Vietnam resolve its problems. The present government, headed by Premier Diem, is confronted by a superhuman task—that of forming a government in a newly independent country, long accustomed to colonial administration and recently split by a military dividing line as a result of the Geneva Accords [signed in July 1954]. The north is occupied by the Communist forces of Ho Chi Minh. At the same time, Saigon has had to provide housing and a means of livelihood for more than 500,000 refugees who have fled the Communist terror in the north—rehabilitate an economy dislocated by war and partition of the country—pacify large areas recently vacated by the Vietminh and still covertly infiltrated with many Vietminh agents—and train a loyal Vietnamese army. . . .

I have mentioned the support of the Bandung communiqué for the collective security principle which is the basis for so much of our effort in Asia. Actually, the implementation of the principle is a complex problem in Asia, for circumstances there have not been readily conducive to the establishment of collective security arrangements. Newly formed nations usually are wary of formal commitments with powers which once held them in colonial control or which they associate with that control. Progress has been made. We have concluded bilateral defense treaties with Japan, Korea, the Philippines, and a trilateral one with Australia and New Zealand. Only very recently a bilateral treaty with the Republic of China has been signed and sealed.

During the period when these various alliances were forming, an event occurred which exerted a powerful leverage in Asia. This was the partition of Vietnam after the defeat of the free forces there which was dramatized by the capitulation of Dienbienphu. The need for collective security became more apparent to all concerned. One result was the eight-nation meeting at Manila [in September 1954], and the Manila Pact and Pacific Charter which emerged from it. The pact . . . binds eight nations, Asian and non-Asian, of Southeast Asia together against direct aggression and indirect subversion as well, and throws a mantle of protection over the new nations of Laos, Cambodia, and southern Vietnam. [Signatories are the United States, Britain, France, Australia, New Zealand, Thailand, Pakistan and the Philippines.]

The Bangkok meeting of the Council of the Manila Pact signatories . . . [in] February [1955] was a first step to put flesh on the bare bones of the pact. In addition to action on the military aspects of the treaty, it was decided that experts would meet soon to discuss ways of improving economic, and social conditions throughout the treaty area.

On the other side of the Asian land mass there is forming the northern tier for the defense of the Middle East—an indigenous effort that is moving forward at a good pace. Turkey and Pakistan, for example, have signed a formal agreement to discuss mutual problems of defense. More recently Turkey and Iraq have joined in a defense pact which Pakistan has been invited to join. We have ourselves reached military aid agreements with Turkey, Pakistan, and Iraq and have a continuing agreement with Iran. . . . Finally, Pakistan is a member of the Manila Pact grouping.

The problem of economic development ranked high on the agenda at Bandung. One of the most important forces in Asia today is the widespread insistence that the Asians, as well as the people of the West, must increasingly enjoy the better life which technical and industrial advancement makes possible.

This your government long ago recognized and took constructive action.

More recently the Communists became aware of this. Speaking in the soft voice of economic betterment, their recent overtures find a response in countries where hunger and poverty are often age-old facts of life or where export markets are a vital necessity to the national well-being. To Ceylon they may say, we will buy your rubber; to Burma, we will buy your rice; to India, we will build you a modern steel plant—which the Indians will pay for—so that you can appreciate the wonders of industrial design and production under communism, and profit thereby.

Asian demand for economic and social betterment is a pivotal point in determining the future political orientation of the peoples of the area. That is why our programs of economic and technical assistance are geared in Asia along with our efforts to assist the Asians in building defenses against aggression.

United States assistance to Asia is not designed simply to counter Communist gestures in that region. We do not see this as a contest to see who can gain the most gratitude. In the first place, Communist gestures toward technical aid to nonindustrial areas are mainly gestures, designed for propaganda effect. Even more importantly, United States efforts to help free nations strengthen themselves are positive efforts; they are good in themselves; they would be right under any circumstances. We are not merely working against something; we are for freedom, the dignity of the individual, and better standards of living everywhere.

One most important point should be kept in mind in thinking about the problem of economic development for the Asians. In contrast to Europe, where the principal task of the Marshall Plan was to restore and regenerate an already existing industrial system, in much of Asia economic development must start at rock bottom. Our programs there must largely emphasize the spread of basic technical skills without which developmental plans can have no effective implementation. Accordingly, our economic assistance programs in Asia are based upon long-range planning in contrast to the relatively short-range, emergency nature of our reconstruction effort in Europe. We will take full advantage of existing regional organizations, such as the Colombo Plan. [See "Using the Colombo Plan" in Section III below.] In addition to our direct assistance, we are trying to help the Asian countries to increase the opportunities for trade with each other and with other free-world countries. . . . Our aid, of course, can only be a supplement and a stimulant to the efforts which the countries themselves will make to achieve more rapid economic development and higher living standards.

Within the general framework of the approach I have indicated, substantial progress already has been made. To illustrate, FOA [Foreign Operations Administration, now succeeded by the International Cooperation Administration] has assisted the Philippines in a material increase in their rice production. In Indonesia our aid is helping to defeat man's tropical enemy— malaria—and increase and improve rice production. As a part of FOA's support of India's development program, some of the local sales proceeds of the aid supplied is being chan- neled, along with private and International Bank funds, to fi- nance the operation of a newly established Industrial Credit and Investment Corporation which, by promoting private in- dustrial development in India, will help generate greater local capital sources for further development. . . .

These are but a few examples of the kind of economic de- velopment programs in which we are engaged in Asia today. With all of the wonderful skill and imagination which have brought such productive power to the United States, we need not fear the competitive influence of the Communist nations in the field of Asian economic development.

COMMUNIST TACTICS [4]

The shooting has stopped in Korea and Indo-China but peace in Southeast Asia has turned out to be "a continuation of war by other means." Preoccupied though it is with industrial construc-

[4] From "Communists Find Asia Ripe for Subversion," news story by Henry R. Lieberman, New York *Times* Hong Kong correspondent. New York *Times*. p E5. December 26, 1954. Reprinted by permission.

tion, Communist China is continuing its efforts to extend its revolution and its power in the Far East.

Unless the Communists are prepared to provoke another war in this region, little or big, the only means open to them in pressing their "struggle" is subversion.

The process of subversion involves the application by the Communists of organizational, infiltrative and propaganda techniques that are not exactly new to them. Nor are they strangers to the kind of divisive tactics they have been using in an attempt to divide the West, lull the Asian neutralists and isolate the United States.

Much of the propaganda fire now emanating from both Peiping and Hanoi radios is being directed against SEATO [Southeast Asia Treaty Organization]. How strong an instrument the Manila pact is remains to be seen but it is reasonably clear that any kind of anti-Communist "united front" approach in Southeast Asia would pose extra difficulties for the Communist camp in this area.

Quite apart from the power at their own disposal the Communists have been assisted by the disunity and political weaknesses confronting them in Southeast Asia. Past experience strongly suggests the likelihood that they will continue their attempts to frustrate any move to bolster this target area.

In a speech to the Chinese Communist Central Committee [in 1954] the party secretary general, Liu Shao-chi, noted that "a fortress is most pregnable from within." Liu was then issuing a warning against the danger of party disunity in China but he was also citing a maxim consistently applied by Communists in their own "struggle" for power.

This "struggle" begins, in fact, with the organization of a tightly knit well-disciplined élite committed to subversion as the basic means of attaining power. In the Far East as in Europe, however, the native Communist parties—whether well developed as in Vietnam or relatively weak as in Thailand—do not encompass the limits of Communist influence.

Behind the indigenous Asian Communist organizations is Communist China. Suspicious as many Asians are about China's actual intentions and disenchanted as some have been after visiting totalitarian China, the Communist propaganda slogans of "anti-colonialism," "anti-feudalism," "national liberation" and "peace" still find fertile ground in Southeast Asia.

Such propaganda remains one of the chief forms of Communist infiltration. It has all the greater impact where the non-Communist administration is either weak, frustrated or corrupt. In effect, the Communists tell the people: "Come over to our side to seek redress and help build a better country."

Asian delegations have been brought to China for conducted tours of factories, schools, nurseries and water-conservation projects. In Saigon, where gambling, prostitution and opium dens flourish, Vietminh agents are collecting Vietnamese intellectuals and leading them into the Vietminh regroupment areas to show them how austerely Communists live in waging revolution.

Although the indigenous Communist parties serve as the hard core, the Communists have been making determined efforts to mobilize non-party intellectuals and community leaders within the framework of their "peace movement." Support of such local leaders paves the way to influence among larger groups.

What happens to a Communist-led "united front" once the Communists take power is illustrated by the monolithic state that has emerged in China. At present, however, the Communist campaign to win over non-Communist intellectuals in Southeast Asia is being conducted on a "united front basis."

Three primary instruments are now available to the Chinese Communists in Southeast Asia: indigenous Communist parties, the controlled "peace movement" and the "overseas Chinese." [There are several million people of Chinese nationality or Chinese descent scattered throughout various Asian countries. The largest overseas Chinese communities are in Thailand and Malaya.—Ed.] While the "overseas Chinese" are looked upon with suspicion in Southeast Asia many—perhaps even a majority —are opposed to the Communists.

The impact of communism has been greatest on the young "overseas Chinese." Hundreds of them are going to China each year for study. But even in the case of young "overseas Chinese" some are going to China for study because of the limited opportunities for higher education in the countries in which they reside.

Looked at from almost any angle the "infiltration" problem in Southeast Asia is basically related to the central problem of Communist China.

In maneuvering its power the Peiping government has coupled the threat of war with propaganda emphasizing "peaceful co-existence" and trade.

While seeking to allay Burmese fear of Chinese intervention, the Peiping regime has created concern in Thailand by its establishment of a "Thai Autonomous Area" in southern Yunnan and its subsequent disclosure that Pridi Phanomyong, a former Thai Premier, is in China. Pridi, whose whereabouts were a mystery for some time before this disclosure, is a left-wing rival of the Thai Premier, Pibul Songgram.

In the meantime, however, Indo-China represents the center of gravity in the Southeast Asian power struggle. Loss of South Vietnam to the Communists would clearly have important repercussions in Laos, Cambodia and Thailand.

The Communist-led Vietminh movement is sufficiently well developed to carry a Vietnamese banner of "national liberation." But it owes its present strength to Chinese Communist support. It is still being assisted by China and it represents the spearhead of the Communist advance in Southeast Asia.

WHAT ASIANS THINK OF US [5]

Once after spending a long, happy time in the Far East it suddenly came to me that none of us Americans had ever discussed one of the really acute questions of relations between Asia and the West. We go around asking ourselves anxiously and ponderously: Are we being properly democratic with these people? What is the best way in which we can show them that our system of government will work for them? But we don't ask: What do Asians think of us?

[5] From "Those Barbaric Americans," article by Emily Hahn, author. *pb: The Pocket Book Magazine.* 1:66-80. November 1954. Reprinted by permission.

We teach them in the kindest manner our methods of hygiene and agriculture and education. We even let them teach us a few things. . . . But one thing we've always avoided thinking about, let alone talking about, is the subject of our cleanliness compared with theirs, and all the horrid little sub-subjects that go along with it. Hundreds of us who have lived in China and Japan and India know perfectly well that Asians do talk about this among themselves, but we wince from admitting it. Asians think we're dirty. They also think we're ignorant and immoral. . . .

Please don't get me wrong. I'm talking in a strictly academic way. I make no suggestion that we really are dirty, or that we ought to dash right off to India and adopt their most stringent Brahman rules, cleansing ourselves all day. I'm just thinking aloud, as they say in Hollywood; setting down facts. It's good exercise to figure out the other man's point of view, just as it's good to see your back view unexpectedly in one of those department-store mirrors when you're trying on a coat.

There is a story, probably apocryphal, about Mme. Pandit and some Americans who asked her about the caste system in India. Mme. Pandit had politely explained the orthodox idea that a Hindu breaks caste by crossing water, and that Hindus returned from overseas have to go through an elaborate rigmarole in order to be reinstated. One of the Americans timorously said, "Now tell me about your Untouchables. The caste system must be very cruel; I've always been so sorry for them. Just what is an Untouchable?"

Mme. Pandit, so the story goes, suddenly laughed out loud. "Why," she said, "you're all Untouchables!"

As I said, it's probably apocryphal. Just the same, it makes you think, doesn't it? . . .

Most tricky of all the difficulties is the fact that we generalize too much on the term "Asians." Logically we haven't any right to do it. India and China are as separate as Europe and America; more so, really, because most of America's population is European in origin, whereas the Indians and the Chinese haven't any common ancestors at all. The Japanese are more complicated, because their chief stock, presumably, is Chinese, but they also have a heavy admixture of Malay blood, and Malays aren't Indian or Chinese by descent. So when we say "Asia" and try to talk about Asians all in a block, we're thinking sloppily.

Almost the only generalization it's safe to make about them is that they all think we're rather peculiar. You may ask, in what way? Well, what do people in any area think of another foreign world? Asians have various sorts of feelings about us, and one of the strongest is resentment of the West because of the long history of colonial expansion. The British had the upper hand in the East for quite a time in most countries of Asia, and Asians' memory of their rule is still green. We Americans come in for some of this resentment whether or not we deserve it. In Siam [Thailand], however, where white people never had much influence or power, there is a different attitude; a kind of cheerful contempt which I think you'd find in the other countries if there had never been what it's now fashionable to call Wicked Imperialism. It is comparable to the way we feel ourselves when we are faced with foreigners who are not like us. No resentment, just incredulous amusement. . . .

The fact is people who live in hot climates take lots more baths than do those in cooler ones, and we Americans wash a good deal more often than the British do, or even the Dutch, because we have such hot summers and live in centrally heated houses in the winter. India is much hotter than the States, and Indians are always sloshing themselves with water. . . .

The Japanese, though they think they have very strict ideas about women's behavior, and consider us terribly immoral for kissing in public, go in for naked mixed bathing. . . . This is why I am always taken aback when Japanese people scold me, no matter how gently, for the unseemly behavior of Westerners who go around holding hands in public with friends of the opposite sex. And as for the kissing! Kissing to the Japanese is just about as intimate as you can get. This is an old story now; everybody knows that kisses have to be cut out of the pictures that go to the East from Hollywood. . . .

When I first went to the East I was told over and over by Westerners that I was going to be shocked by the way Asians treat animals. And I was shocked. They seemed to have no imagination at all about animals' suffering, though the Chinese are very kind to pet birds and fish, and the Japanese make beautiful paintings of cats and monkeys. It was heartbreaking to see starved dogs slinking around the villages, and underfed, overworked horses wherever horses were used. It took me all these years to find out the other side of the medal.

"What we really think is perfectly disgusting about foreigners," a Chinese girl said to me last fall, "is the way you let animals eat off the same plates you use, sometimes, and even take them to bed with you. Ugh!" . . .

There is something else that shocks Asians just as badly as our animal worship, if not more so. They think we are perfectly horrible to our old people. In Asian countries—this is one case in which we can safely generalize—the older your parents get, the more you honor them and the bossier they are permitted to become. Asians see how we treat our old fathers and mothers, putting them into "homes" or supporting them in little apartments where they live alone, and they are genuinely scandalized. It is no use trying to explain, as I often do, that our old people feel independent and that a lot of them actually prefer to live alone. In Asia you always keep the old people with you in your house. It is a sacred duty and nothing must interfere with your carrying it out—not convenience, nor financial necessity, nor your own wish, nor the old folks' wish. It just doesn't look right for your parents not to live with you. To let them go elsewhere is indescribably shocking. Asians feel so strongly about this that it's hard to make them talk about it. But when they do, they say a mouthful. . . .

Asians think we are all very rich. With our expense accounts and our advantageous rate of exchange, we usually behave in their countries as if we are, so the mistake is natural. Actually, as somebody pointed out recently in a long-overdue article on the subject, we aren't really that much better off. Just as we have a lot of things Asians consider luxuries, they have things we couldn't possess for less than a large amount of money which are not considered luxuries in the East—handmade articles, quick and accurate repairs, plenty of fruit, lots of inexpensive domestic labor.

They also think we are terribly wasteful, and so we are. Their dislike of our wastefulness is purely on principle, for in practice their poor people benefit from our lavish habits. What we discard is grabbed and used; the only really harmful waste, they think, occurs when we destroy things we don't want any longer. They feel contempt for us, however, and get pleasure out of the feeling of superiority our wastefulness evokes.

The cry of the Westerner dealing with the East has long been "Democracy!" and this, I feel, is not only inevitable, but a good thing. You can't export an idea unless you really believe in it, and our belief in democracy has given us a lot of the sap and fervor that our religion seems to have lost, perhaps only temporarily. Before we dive too deeply into the joys of spreading the light, however, it might be as well to ask the recipients of the light just what they think of it.

We start out on the assumption that they agree with us in wanting freedom. This seems axiomatic, and yet it is not necessarily the case. Most Indians who have been to the West, or to Western-type schools, do indeed want freedom in our exact sense of the word, especially freedom of speech. After all, India was unified and governed—it was even invented as an entity—by Britain, and it is natural that India's literate classes should have adopted British ideals as they adopted Shakespeare and Milton. But not all Indians, even among the literates, agree that freedom of thought and so forth are the most important things the human soul can have. I don't intend to attempt explaining what they *do* want; I just point this out as a reminder that not everyone has the same point of view.

The Chinese were not occupied and schooled by the British and their experience of Western ideals has thus been narrower. Until Sun Yat-sen brought Western ideas home and started expounding them to the people, they had never thought of wanting the sort of freedom we take for granted. Democracy that is not political—democracy of custom—is a different thing. The Chinese in their way are truly democratic in their lack of caste system, their claim that all Chinese are of good blood, and so on. Their aristocracy, in fact, is rather like the American in being founded on wealth rather than blood. (This applies, of course, only to pre-Communist China. I don't know what direction their snobberies take nowadays.) But they were used to being told what to do, and they had hardly learned what it meant to vote before the Communists took over the country. Nevertheless they had been well tutored in the theory of democracy. Perhaps they won't forget. Perhaps our propaganda may work. I don't know.

The Japanese know more about the politics we preach, and in the old days before the war our preaching annoyed them. They saw that we were inconsistent in our treatment of them, and they may have resented it more, if possible, than the Chinese did, because the Chinese had a considerable amount of conceit that made them impervious to certain snubs the Japanese would not ignore. However, it's a moot point really as to which Asian nation we used to offend the most.

For generations the British have been telling Americans that Asians like them best because they know how to handle the chaps. We Americans have retorted that it isn't so; that they like us best because we're so democratic. In the warmth of the argument neither Britons nor Americans seemed to have observed that the doors of our clubs were closed to Asians. Then along came the Soviet Russians, who did open their club doors. They implied to the British and Americans, in print, that the Asians really liked them alone among all foreigners because they practice true democracy and ours is clearly *ersatz*.

Actually, Asians don't like Russians either. They don't like anybody but themselves. As I said before, they are just people, with the usual human reactions. In spreading our kind of light we will get on faster, I think, if we look straight at the facts and take it as settled that none of them really like foreigners at all.

II. THE ARC OF FREE ASIA

EDITOR'S INTRODUCTION

The countries of free Asia have many problems in common—poverty, lack of industrialization, land problems, illiteracy. They also have great diversities, different forms of government, different religions, important disputes among themselves.

To be successful, American policies must be fashioned to take into account both common problems and the individual differences of each nation. And the American public, debating the wisdom of our foreign policy, can only offer constructive support or criticism when there is an awareness of the complexities of the Asian scene.

The following section takes the arc of free Asia country by country, presenting articles that explain why India's policy is what it is, why Pakistan thinks differently, how the Philippines met the challenge of Communist subversion, and so forth. Some aspects of American policy in different countries—our information program in Burma, our military aid to Korea, for instance—are also described.

1. *India*

NEHRU AND INDEPENDENCE [1]

The foreign policy of India, often called "neutralist," has been puzzling and annoying to many in the West. But the principles that guide India have been plainly stated by its spokesmen, and India's actions have been entirely consistent with those principles. On this basis India's attitude in a given situation can be accurately predicted.

[1] From *India Since Independence*, pamphlet by Robert Trumbull, New York *Times* correspondent in India for seven years, now stationed in Tokyo. (Headline Series no 105) Foreign Policy Association. New York. May-June 1954. p46-9, 54-5. Reprinted by permission.

The administrator of India's foreign policy is Prime Minister Nehru, who is also foreign minister. He, in turn, is faithful to the ideals adopted long ago in the field of foreign relations by the Congress party. As early as 1925 the Congress had established the four cardinal points that determine India's path in world affairs today. These are (1) opposition to imperialism and colonial rule, (2) support of subject peoples and oppressed races in their struggle for freedom and equality, (3) promotion of peace and abhorrence of war, and (4) avoidance of foreign entanglements. As former Ambassador Bowles points out in his excellent book on India, *Ambassador's Report,* India's basic foreign policy is indistinguishable from that of the United States until very recent years.

Sometimes India's close adherence to these guiding principles may cause it to minimize a point that is the paramount consideration in the minds of other powers. For instance, it has been said that Nehru is so opposed to French colonialism in Indo-China that he overlooks the greater menace of communism, which imposes a far worse form of colonialism on subject peoples. In his anxiety to promote peace Nehru may occasionally appear to be an appeaser of communism. His very attitude toward "foreign entanglements" results in actions that appear to keep India from joining the rest of the free world in a united front against a common danger. His abhorrence of war and fear of expanding the area of conflict between the democracies and the Communist bloc often place him in the position of seeming to impede the efforts of other free nations to achieve collective security.

It should be realized at the outset, however, that the Congress is bound to oppose the spread of communism by force. If the people of a country want communism—and Indians are quite aware that no Communist regime anywhere has come to power through a free vote—then Indians say, "Let them have it; but we don't want it here, nor do we want communism or any other form of government imposed upon any people against their will." Early in World War II the Congress Working Committee said for the Indian people, "Their sympathy is entirely on the side of democracy and freedom . . . they have a deep-rooted quarrel with systems which deny freedom and are based on violence and aggression."

If India refrains from forthright condemnation of Communist Russia's expansionism, as the Congress party condemned Nazi Germany's rape of smaller countries, notably Czechoslovakia, it is because Nehru feels that hot words only beget hotter words and bring the world closer to war. But when confronted with an outright Communist aggression in Korea, India unhesitatingly joined other powers in supporting a United Nations resolution branding North Korea as the aggressor. When the North Koreans were driven out of the territory they had invaded, India then felt that the objective of the United Nations action had been attained. Nehru warned that crossing of the thirty-eighth parallel would bring Red China into the war, a development which would cost a great many more lives and postpone for an indefinite time any hope of world peace. Events have proved that he was right on that point, whatever else may be said in support of the UN action.

Nehru once pointed out in a memorable conversation with this writer that the objectives of India and the United States are the same but that the two countries are trying to reach them by different roads. Now that the United States has learned by bitter experience the cost of unpreparedness, the American way is to meet force with force. India, having no illusions about its own military weakness, is reluctant to expose itself to reprisal by stronger powers, which it might invite by joining the American-sponsored collective security program.

When analyzing India's actions in the cold war two things should be borne in mind: First, India's own interest is paramount with India, as ours is with us; second, India is still remote from the firing line, and in the press of its vast domestic problems it does not view certain international developments with the same urgency as we, who are the target of Russia and communism.

Americans should clearly understand that India will resort to armed force when it conceives that its interests are sufficiently threatened. Since independence India has sent troops into action in Kashmir, Hyderabad, Junagadh, Sikkim and Nepal. Nehru adopted a strong tone toward Communist China when Mao's troops entered peaceful autonomous Tibet. When Peiping told him to mind his own business and said he was an imperialist stooge, there was nothing concrete that Nehru could do. Because of his desire to conciliate a frighteningly powerful neighbor he has since been rationalizing the situation in his public references to Tibet, but India's defenses have been strengthened along the border and Nehru has stated bluntly that India's army would fight if there were any incursion, from any quarter, into India or the territory of the neighboring kingdom of Nepal. He also helped Nepal put down local uprisings that were thought to be Communist inspired.

Many Americans believe that Nehru, in attempting to walk a middle path between East and West, is following a course of dangerous neutrality between good and evil. In the first place, Nehru does not consider India neutral when any such choice is to be made, and he so assured the United States Congress on his visit to Washington in 1949. He does speak of "dynamic neutrality," which could be interpreted to mean "neutral on the side of democracy," although some Americans choose to construe it the opposite way. On analysis, however, it appears that while Nehru is often critical of American methods, he is in full sympathy with Washington's motives. He just thinks we sometimes go about things the wrong way.

Since the British left India the United States has inherited the suspicion with which a former colonial people regard the most powerful nation they know. "India has had a bellyful of powerful nations," a distinguished Indian editor once explained. "We distrust them on general principles." Why is there not equal distrust of Russia, which is powerful, predatory, and much nearer? Many Indians, when confronted with this question, reply that India does not know Russia so well and feels freer to criticize the United States as a tolerant old friend with whom it is on good terms. At this the baffled American usually shakes his head and changes the subject. . . .

Nehru frequently admits differences in point of view between democratic India and Communist China but endeavors to main-

tain relations on the friendliest possible plane. The current interchange between India and China on the political and cultural
levels is a new thing in recent centuries and could turn out to be
a significant development of our time. Actually the two countries
have little in common beyond a background of foreign exploitation and consequent suspicion of colonialism and the West. On
India's side, there is an uncomfortable realization of China's overwhelming military might and of the potentialities for Communist
expansionism in the new combination of China and Russia on
the Indian border.

Nehru's policy toward Communist China is apparently moti-
vated by a desire to see Peiping break away from Russian influence. He is convinced that this will eventually happen. In fact, he
believes that even today there is more concern over China in
Moscow than in Washington. He asserts that the United States,
by opposing Communist China's entry into the United Nations
and otherwise isolating this great Asian power, tends to drive the
Peiping rulers closer to the Kremlin.

An important additional factor in India's sponsorship of Communist China's case for admission to the UN is Nehru's conviction that the effectiveness of the world body is vitiated by the ex-
clusion of a nation that contains nearly a quarter of the globe's
population. He is also disturbed to see that all Asia is represented
permanently on the UN Security Council by the Nationalist Chinese government, which he contends can speak only for the island
of Formosa, if that. Finally, Nehru does not believe that the
United Nations can function effectively as a forum for the settlement of disputes if one of the principal parties has no voice in
its deliberations.

India and the United States, as the two largest democracies,
are unfortunately at odds from time to time over methods of
procedure in attaining common ideals. The area of conflict might
be lessened if more Americans had a clearer understanding of
the Indian point of view. Without such understanding there is
little prospect of achieving the sympathetic relationship that
history and mutual interests suggest.

AN UNSENTIMENTAL LOOK AT INDIA [2]

"It looks different from New Delhi" is the standard comment with which Prime Minister Pandit Nehru greets Western visitors. Indeed it does. The gap between India and America is growing fast—and nearly all Indians, plus a good many sentimental Americans, put the blame entirely on the United States. They accuse us of failure to "understand the Eastern mind"; and they often talk a good deal about the "spiritual qualities" of the Orient and the noble character of Nehru. Rarely is there any hint that Indians might fail to understand America, or to appreciate the spiritual qualities of the West.

When I returned recently from ten strenuous weeks in India, I was convinced that misunderstanding is by no means a one-way street. As I visited universities, research institutions, and government agencies, I found myself under the constant provocation of challenging argument, misinformation, inverted racism—and a searching curiosity about America. Since I was a private visitor, with no official responsibilities, I could afford to give frank answers, which often collided head on with the established stereotypes of Indian thought.

For example, the audiences at my lectures were always startled when I reminded them that America had been drawn into World War II because an Asiatic power had attacked us. They have swallowed so much anti-colonial propaganda, which invariably casts "Europeans" in the role of aggressors, that they could hardly credit the fact of Pearl Harbor. (A minor, but curious, item of misunderstanding is the way in which Indians normally use the term "European" for all Westerners, including Americans; but it does not seem to include the Russians.) Moreover, when I pointed out the reason for Japan's attack— the fact that America was the only consistent defender of China against Japanese aggression—my listeners often seemed to feel that I was inventing a debater's argument. The historical truth simply did not fit their preconceptions.

The remark that "it looks different from New Delhi" often is accompanied by a rather smug assumption that India has a

[2] From article by Harry D. Gideonse, president of Brooklyn College. *Harper's Magazine.* 208:78-9, 83. June 1954. Reprinted by permission.

monopoly on virtue, and that it alone presents "the Asiatic viewpoint." Yet Nehru obviously does not speak for Red China—nor for Formosa. New Delhi doesn't speak for Japan either; it doesn't even think of Japan. In Indian minds, the Japan of the past is somehow curiously merged with the responsibilities of the British; and the Japan of the present and future is confused with the responsibilities of the United States. When an American points out that Communist aggression in Korea was essentially aimed at Japan—and notes that Japan therefore is more concerned with the future of Korea than India is—his Indian listeners seem to freeze. Similarly, I observed repeatedly that the Indian press simply ignores official American statements which stress the Japanese interest in a Korean settlement.

The gap between New Delhi and Washington is not caused merely by geography or a different memory of recent experiences. It is also—and overwhelmingly so, in my experience—a matter of different ideals, and of startlingly divergent ways of expressing such ideals.

The key word in American information activities—and in our political pronouncements—is "freedom." We are always speaking of the "free world" and of "freedom" as if these were self-evident truths, as clear to any listener in India as they would be to a Middle Western newspaper reader. They may make some sense to the small group of Westernized, educated Indians, but even to this small segment of the three hundred and sixty million people who live in the subcontinent, the terms are confusing.

In Calcutta I was invited to lecture on "Changing American Philosophies of Freedom" to a large Hindu group. The audience was apparently deeply interested, and there were many questions in the stifling heat of an Indian summer afternoon. But I was amazed by one question toward the end of the two-hour session. It started with the characteristically flowery courtesy of the East, but ended with the blunt statement that the audience had listened for two hours to interesting "Atlantica" but had "heard nothing about the subject that had been announced, since there had not been a word said about the soul."

That evening at my hotel, in the rare comfort of an air-conditioned room, I was initiated by a professor of Sanskrit into the difficulties of translating the conception—and even the word —of freedom into the languages of India. There is a word that means self-government. There is another word that means autonomy. But the word "freedom" in my lecture topic was probably understood as the equivalent of *moksha*, which is usually rendered as "freedom" in the classical Hindu sense that "freedom is the absence of desire." That is the way, for instance, in which it is used in the Bhagavad-Gita, the holy epic of Hinduism. The word is related to the liberation of the self from material or physical needs, and it is obviously almost the exact opposite of our conception of freedom as the presence of choice. Choice is clearly rooted in desire—or, at least, in interest.

In succeeding versions of the same lecture, I found common ground by discussing the Henry David Thoreau part of our tradition. I also stressed the difficulties which India was encountering in its economic development plans, because higher standards of living, industrialization, and capital investment are all based on moral principles which are the opposite of the traditional Hindu ideal of renunciation.

But our traditional American stress on "freedom," as related to the economic phases of the "American way," almost certainly misses fire in India. The attempt to appeal to Indians by using the psychological assumptions of a modern American advertising agency frequently clashes with the classical Indian conception of freedom which regards the satisfying of material wants—including sanitation—as essentially "busy work."

And this conflict in basic motives—the desire for increased productivity, on the one hand, and the admiration for religious renunciation on the other—is the deepest and the most tragic dilemma facing the leaders of modern India. There are a few Indian intellectuals who are giving careful attention to the problem of restating India's cultural and spiritual traditions in a manner compatible with India's material needs. Moreover, Nehru's ambivalent and obsolete position on these issues is widely criticized within the Congress party. But usually the gap is filled with "leftist" slogans which beg the moral question, while they suggest that material productivity is largely a question of scientific magic. This fashionable "leftist thinking" also implies that capital development will fall from the skies like manna, rather than grow from concerted productive effort.

As a skillful politician, Nehru may sometimes criticize the West for internal political reasons. Sometimes he may speak for the effect on Moscow and Peiping, using the West much as Roosevelt used Churchill at Yalta in the hope of winning Stalin's confidence. Nehru doesn't regard the United States as designedly imperialistic and knows Roosevelt's role in promoting the freedom of India and other Asian colonial peoples. However, even his friends acknowledge there is a vein of anti-Americanism in him. It has been attributed to his English governess and his education at Harrow and Cambridge at a time when many Englishmen looked down their noses at us. It is said he was rubbed the wrong way by ostentation of some of his hosts during his American visit six years ago. Whatever its origins, the vein is there. Since he has a penchant for candor, is emotional, and speaks without notes, the vein shows more than it would if he were always a calculating diplomat.

Nevertheless, Nehru unquestionably desires our friendship and appreciates our economic aid. Since its independence, India's progress has been substantial, in some ways astonishing. One senses a release of tremendous vitality. But India must go far to reach a solid economic and social footing.

As a thorough democrat schooled in great liberal traditions, Nehru is fundamentally anti-Communist. In India, he is effectively anti-Communist. When the Reds resorted to violence a few years ago he sent them to jail by the wagonload. With the help of tough practical organizers in the Congress party, he has whipped them at the polls, most recently in Andhra, where the Communists had concentrated on building a base among the landless poor peasants. Nehru is making democracy work in a nation of 360 million, most of whom are still illiterate. No other man in the world leads so many people with their free assent.

His attacks on the West abet Communist world objectives, however. An independent foreign policy for India alone would

not be troublesome even though we consider that Nehru's equat-
ing of two power blocs is morally blind. The real difficulty arises
from his efforts to line up Asia in a third bloc. This would be
helpful if it were a bloc of strength in which India assumed responsibility for the defense of its neighbors as well as herself.
But Nehru's prescription is a bloc of military weakness. If successful, this would leave free Asia defenseless against overt
aggression.

NEHRU AND US: SOME ADVICE [3]

There is more good will toward the United States in India
than might be supposed from Prime Minister Nehru's periodic
castigations of our policy. There would be still more if he
stopped criticizing the United States.

Nehru says some nice things about us now and then. More
than once he has voiced his conviction that President Eisenhower
is a man of peace. Also, he keeps telling his own people that the
Communist way is not theirs because it means loss of freedom,
and once in a while he publicly admonishes Moscow or Peiping.
But his criticisms of the democratic West often seem inexplicable
for a man who treasures democracy and freedom.

I arrived in the Indian capital immediately after Nehru had
given the West a bitter lashing before the lower house of Parliament. Well-informed Indians, including three high officials, said
or implied they felt personally that his criticism had been exces-
sively severe and attributed it to a surge of emotion. When I
asked what had made him emotional, the causes most frequently
cited were: The refusal of leading Western nations to denounce
race policies in the Union of South Africa; resentment at Western
intrusion into Asian affairs, especially through the Manila pact
and encouragement of the Turko-Iraqi-Pakistani alliance; and the
feeling that we had stupidly blundered by ignoring his advice in
the past—for example, by crossing the thirty-eighth parallel in
Korea.

[3] By Ernest K. Lindley, *Newsweek* Washington columnist who toured Asia in
the spring of 1955. *Newsweek* 45:38. April 25, 1955. Reprinted by permission.

2. *Pakistan*

DIVIDED IT STANDS [4]

There is nothing under the sun quite like the new, enormously vigorous, fiercely independent state of Pakistan. The seventh largest country on earth and the most important Moslem nation, it is a geographic freak. The country is divided into two parts separated from each other by a thousand miles of India. But new as it is, and divided as it will always be, Pakistan is a brightly hopeful spot on the darkening map of Asia. It is our strong new friend.

Pakistan is the world's first nation to have been conceived by a poet. This was Mohammed Iqbal, who wrote mystic poems foretelling a new Moslem nation that would arise in British India. Then in 1940, a whip-sharp patriot named Mohammed Ali Jinnah caught the vision. Seven years later, when India gained independence, Pakistan was born.

The new nation was founded on purely religious principles. British India contained a large Moslem minority who with fierce determination guarded the religion handed down to them by the Prophet Mohammed. When the Moslems finally gained a separate state they boldly wrote in their constitution: "The entire universe belongs to God Almighty, and the authority which He has delegated to the State of Pakistan is a sacred trust."

When the country was launched foreign offices around the world thought it might last six months, then fall back into India. Editors of one world-wide news service were advised by the boss "not to bother with Pakistan because next year it won't be around." Sure enough, disaster struck immediately.

The rules whereby Pakistan was formed were drawn by the British in great haste. Partition from India was announced for the first time on June 3, 1947; seventy-two days later an entire subcontinent was divided up and Pakistan was on its own. It

[4] From "Pakistan: Divided It Stands," article by James A. Michener, author of *Tales of the South Pacific* and other works, both fiction and nonfiction, dealing with Asia. *Reader's Digest.* 65:136-46. November 1954. Reprinted by permission.

is an amazing fact that the government was in operation three days before it was told what its boundaries were.

Then began what historians call "the greatest interchange of population in history." Hindus whose homes were now in Moslem Pakistan understandably wanted to move over the line to India. Moslems felt the same way about joining Pakistan. Accordingly, more than 12 million people set out, mostly on foot, to seek their new homeland.

The vast exodus occurred in the middle of a blazing summer. Many of the lands to be crossed were desert. The human suffering was incalculable and thousands perished. But terrible religious riots also broke out and at least half a million travelers were massacred.

Bullock carts were halted and all occupants were slashed to death. Trains to which some fled for protection were dynamited and every passenger slain. At river banks, where the fleeing millions piled up, gangs of inflamed men with knives ripped throats until the river was stained. It is thought that more than a hundred thousand young women were kidnaped, never to be seen again. Today no one tries to assess blame for this enormous crime. Indians and Pakistanis alike were engulfed in the fury of the moment.

Moslems who survived assassination swept down upon a Pakistan ill-equipped to receive them. Karachi, the new capital, started with a population of about 300,000. Soon it contained over 1.5 million. Its water, electricity, sewer and public-health systems could not accommodate such masses. It has been estimated that in the first terrible winter four million people throughout Pakistan were without homes. They slept in gutters. They foraged in garbage. They died of cold in the north and of blazing sun in the south. . . .

The accomplishment of these early years is unbelievable, for the Moslems were poorly equipped to run a nation of their own, having few trained leaders. But those they had worked overtime. New industries were set up. National credit was established. New markets were found. And, with the help of British generals, one of the finest armies in Asia was whipped into shape.

In the Pakistani army, the United States has a first-class ally. There is no draft in Pakistan, but there have been two serious and unusual recruitment problems. Sons of men who for three generations have served in the army insist upon enlisting at the age of 12 or 13. (Separate academies have been set aside for them.) And the original enlistment period had to be extended to a term of 15 years "because boys thought anything less wasn't really worth-while." In many villages no self-respecting girl will marry anyone but a soldier.

A strong central government and a dependable army saved Pakistan.

Then a new series of disasters rocked the nation. The prime minister was murdered by a crazy man. The world price for jute and cotton collapsed. Pakistan nearly went bankrupt.

Again the rugged Pakistanis rallied. After one false start they found an aggressive and courageous prime minister. Young Mohammed Ali is a big, good-looking man in his 40's, the youngest leader of any major nation. He has served as High Commissioner in Canada and as Ambassador to Washington. In extensive motor trips throughout America he sized up American capacities. When he was called home to lead his nation he surrounded himself with a remarkably young cabinet and announced his belief in many things he had learned in North America. Quickly he concluded a military-aid pact with the United States.

The bravery required for such an act can be appreciated only by looking at the map. Only a twelve-mile strip separates Pakistan from Russia on the north and, should America fail to come through with aid, Pakistan could be easily invaded. That was the risk Mohammed Ali took. [Mohammed Ali resigned as prime minister in August 1955 after Pakistan's first elections. He was succeeded by his former finance minister, a man with a somewhat similar name—Chaudhri Mohammed Ali.—Ed.]. . .

The awful problem of overpopulation can best be described this way. East Pakistan is just about the size of Wisconsin. But East Pakistan contains 42 million people. Wisconsin has only 3.4 million and the soil of Wisconsin grows more food!

Fortunately, West Pakistan (34 million people in an area larger than Texas) produces an astonishing amount of food. The Indus River, along whose shores civilization thrived at the time of the glory of Babylon, runs through what was once a vast desert. It is joined by a complex of five rivers—Punjab means Land of Five Rivers—which are interconnected by a series of amazing canals. Some date back to prehistoric times and still function. Others were the work of devoted British experts. Some are as new as last year. . . .

The canal system of the Punjab has long been a testimonial to man's common sense. Today it is a monument to his stupidity. For the line separating India from Pakistan cuts right across the middle of this complex system. All the rivers that feed the Pakistani canals are controlled by India, as are the gates to many canals upon which Pakistan must depend for existence. It is no figure of speech to state that India has the power of life and death over Pakistan.

Luckily, India realizes the cruel responsibility handed to it by the commission which drew the boundary lines. Some kind of international agreement, possibly sponsored by the World Bank, must be worked out to insure just allocation of the river waters. Nevertheless, as long as Pakistan exists, India will have the power to starve her. If there ever was an international situation requiring tact and forbearance it is this.

Obviously, the bitterness of partition, followed by the massacres, made relations between India and Pakistan difficult. At first each side threatened war, but gradually minor differences have been ironed out in honest good will. Tariffs and passport regulations have been adjusted. Today . . . [these] major problems remain: . . . the water situation has not been settled; nor the future of Kashmir.

Since Kashmir is overwhelmingly Moslem, Pakistan wants it. Since it is strategically important to India, Nehru insists upon it. Three years ago it seemed as if only war could solve the impasse. Today intelligent and fair-minded people in each country are determined to find some peaceful solution.

Pakistan feels that in each of these disputes the next step must come from India, the more powerful of the two nations. (Pakistan has 76 million people, India 357 million.). . .

Most Pakistani peasants live in sun-baked mud villages at near-starvation levels. Average income is about $80 a year. Families are large, needs are many. Few children get a chance to go to school and the nation remains 80 per cent illiterate. But village life is good, bound together tightly by tradition, humor and hope. Under the new government, schools are becoming common and income is rising. . . .

Pakistanis are convinced that because they are Moslems, communism will never be a threat in their country. This is daydreaming. If the government does not work hard to insure social justice, communism will make deep inroads. After all, the Prophet Mohammed and the poet Iqbal were revolutionaries. They preached a stalwart doctrine of equality. Should the government of Pakistan ignore the uncomfortable parts of their teaching, the citizens of Pakistan will look elsewhere.

Pakistan, of all the major Asiatic nations, is most tardy in its land reform. There is still a great deal of absentee landlordism. Steps have been taken in the Punjab, but the government is hesitant when boldness is required.

Pakistan's most urgent problem, of course, concerns the job of holding the two separate parts together in a strong federal union. . . . [In 1954] riots and political uprisings in East Pakistan showed that this great problem will not be entirely solved for a long time. But all sensible Pakistani officials work toward binding the two parts together. A healthy tradition has grown up that neither the East nor the West should ever provide both the president and the prime minister to the central government. For seven years cynics have been predicting that East Pakistan would break away from West. Overlooked is the fact that East Pakistan led the fight for independence, that her people prosper today compared with yesterday under Hindu rule, and that a separate nation consisting only of East Pakistan would be economically impossible.

AN ASIAN FRIEND OF OURS [5]

Americans are cordially welcomed here. Alone among the new nations of South Asia, Pakistan has emphatically rejected neutralism and taken an unequivocal stand against Communist expansion. It is proud to be an ally of the United States through the Manila pact and to have taken the lead with Turkey in forming a top-tier defense in the Middle East. It wants more than an alliance with us. It seeks a close, friendly relationship.

Pakistan is grateful for our military and economic aid—and doubtless will be still more grateful when more of the aid promised actually arrives. For the long pull, however, it wants American private investment. Its internal policies encourage private enterprise and it has adopted laws designed to attract capital and experienced management from abroad. The response from United States business is disappointing, but Pakistan is hoping for concrete results in the near future.

Pakistan is working its way out of an internal constitutional and political snarl. The parliamentary government in East Pakistan was suspended last year. Now the National Constituent Assembly—the old legislative body formed at the beginning of its national existence—has been abolished. By decree, all of West Pakistan is being united into a single province. The Pakistani with whom I talked here evinced concern lest the interruption of democratic processes and difficulties which caused it weaken American confidence in Pakistan's future. Actually, the leadership is in strong hands. The constitution probably will soon be promulgated. . . .

When I was here six and a half years ago, shortly after the birth of Pakistan, obstacles to creating a viable nation looked almost insuperable. Each of the widely separated halves was purely agricultural. Karachi was flooded with Moslem refugees from India. . . .

Since then Pakistan has made substantial progress. Some of it strikes the eye as the plane flies over Karachi toward the air-

    [5] By Ernest K. Lindley, Washington columnist for *Newsweek*. *Newsweek*. 45:48. April 18, 1955. Reprinted by permission.

port. The city has expanded greatly, nearly trebling its housed population. Pakistan is near its initial economic goal: Self-sufficiency in production of the essentials of life.

Basic development work under way ranges from large-scale irrigation projects to improvements in farm methods and village life. Coal production has doubled, Standard Vacuum is hunting for oil, and the government hopes that exploration will find other minerals as a base for heavy industry.

Pakistan's foreign earnings, largely from jute and cotton, slumped with the end of the Korean war. At the same time, capital development and needs for more raw materials for new industries have increased imports. United States aid to the tune of $110 million this fiscal year is a life saver.

Pakistan will need the flow of American dollars for a long time to come, but its leaders hope that a large part will come through investment by American business. Chaudhri Mohammed Ali, capable [former] Minister of Finance and Economic Affairs [and now prime minister], talks about private enterprise's role in a manner to delight the heart of Treasury Secretary George M. Humphrey.

Inescapably, we have a stake in the success of this Moslem nation of nearly 80 million people. The stake was there before the Manila pact, but through this alliance our prestige is, to some extent, involved. Happily, despite obvious difficulties in converting Pakistan into a strong modern nation, it is involved with self-respecting people of great resolution.

3. *Ceylon*

AN ASIAN LEADER SPEAKS UP [6]

Sir John Kotelawala, 58, Ceylon's Prime Minister, is a man Nehru tends to patronize, and others to underrate. A neutralist, he first conceived the idea of the Colombo powers (India, Pakistan, Burma, Indonesia and Ceylon), the group of ex-colonies

[6] From "A Member Poses a Question." *Time.* 65:28. May 2, 1955. Courtesy *Time* Magazine; copyright Time, Inc. 1955.

who won their independence after World War II and banded together this year to sponsor the conference at Bandung. Though he opposes SEATO [Southeast Asia Treaty Organization] and wishes Chiang Kai-shek would exile himself from Formosa, Sir John insists that "there is no purpose in standing neutral for the benefit of the wrong party." On a tour of the United States last year, he told everyone from President Eisenhower on down that he believes "in self-help and development for Asia— not handouts."

A member of one of Ceylon's patrician families, Sir John is strong-minded, wealthy (coconut groves and graphite mines) and sometimes unpredictable. . . . [After becoming prime minister in 1953] Kotelawala proved the quality of his anti-communism. He (1) ordered the Bank of Ceylon to stop payment on funds for Communists coming in from Russia; (2) drafted stiff new penalties, with fourteen years imprisonment for political subverters; (3) turned down a request from Red China for a good-will mission to Ceylon, saying: "We sell you rubber, you sell us rice. Ceylon has no other friendship or dealing with Communist China. Nor does she want it."

Other proven friends of the West (Turkey, Iraq, Pakistan, Thailand, the Philippines) spoke effectively for the West at Bandung. The significance of Sir John Kotelawala's speech was that it came from a neutralist, who, perceiving the bogus neutrality of Nehru's anti-colonialism, clearly redefined the issue. Excerpts:

All of us here, I take it, are against colonialism, but let us be equally unanimous and positive in declaring to the world that we are unanimous in our opposition to all forms of colonialism. Colonialism takes many forms. Think, for example, of those satellite states under Communist domination in Central and Eastern Europe—of Hungary, Rumania, Bulgaria, Albania, Czechoslovakia, Latvia, Lithuania, Estonia and Poland. Are these not colonies as much as any of the colonial territories in Africa? If we are united in our opposition to colonialism, should it not be our duty to declare our opposition to Soviet colonialism as much as to Western imperialism? Our friends from China might want to clarify the doubts.

It has been the experience of most countries in this part of the world that the local Communist parties regard themselves as agents of the great Communist powers of Russia and China. They make no bones about it—why should we?

In my country, for example, the local Communist party has been so bold as to declare openly that, if there were a war in which Ceylon found herself on one side and Russia and China on the other, the Communists in Ceylon would do everything in their power including fighting, to promote the victory of Russia and China and the defeat of Ceylon.

If the Communist powers are in earnest about their professions of their desire for peaceful coexistence, how should they react to such a declaration? I am aware that the stock answer to this is that the Communist parties concerned are autonomous bodies which do not take their orders from any foreign power. If this is so, then China would have nothing to lose and would gain immeasurably with all of us in prestige by publicly and formally calling upon the local Communist groups throughout Asia and Africa to disband. This reassuring gesture from Peiping has not been forthcoming, and I for one am perturbed about it.

In the light of such tactics, how is it possible for non-Communist countries to regard coexistence as a possibility, still less a reality? How can we regard coexistence as anything but a snare and a delusion until such time as the Cominform is dissolved? Here again our friends of the Communist camp have a ready answer. They say it is Russia that controls the Cominform, and what can China do about it? This argument leaves room for doubt as to whether there is perhaps a division of labor between the two great Communist powers, and that the role of China might be to look on smiling while Russia does the dirty work.

If this doubt is unreasonable and uncharitable, we should have expected China to exert every possible influence upon Russia—I am persuaded that her influence in that quarter is by no means negligible —and we should have expected this to be done openly and in the eyes of the world. It has not been done openly. It has not been done at all.

Coexistence implies, and indeed necessitates the total noninterference by any power in the affairs of another. Coexistence means to live and let live. I cannot for the life of me understand why we should be expected only to let live, while we ignore the threats to our own life and institutions.

4. Burma

U NU AND HIS WATCHFUL NATION [7]

The prime minister of this never-never land [Burma] is a short, cheerful man who has passed his forty-eighth birthday without acquiring a line in his round, brown face. U Nu—the

[7] From "Man on a Rickety Fence," article by Robert Sherrod, managing editor of the *Saturday Evening Post*. *Saturday Evening Post*. 227:26-7+. April 23, 1955. Reprinted by permission.

"U" approximates mister; both the title and the name rhyme with "woo"—is ordinarily not given to worrying. He is apt to quote, as he did before a convention of Burma Baptists one day last fall, a saying long popular in this Buddhist country, "The sky will not drop, and what if it does?"

There is some evidence, nevertheless, that Prime Minister Nu has of late fallen to worrying. He is disturbed by the warlike clouds that hang darkly over the globe and most likely would spill on Asia first. The hostility between the United States and Communist China, he feels, is "far more intense" than the pre-World War II tension between the Axis and the Anglo-American alliance. U Nu wants to do something to relieve this tension, and he offers himself as a peacemaker: "I pray that the United States and the People's Republic of China may be able to work jointly and with understanding for world peace and progress."

Americans tend to think of Burma in terms of Kipling's *The Road to Mandalay,* where the wind blows through the palm trees and tinkles the temple bells; in terms of the Burma Road and Merrill's Marauders, and of Vinegar Joe Stilwell saying "I claim we took a hell of a beating," or perhaps of a shaving cream advertised alongside innumerable American roadsides—but not on sale in Burma. Until U Nu first suggested himself as a peacemaker, I never heard Burma mentioned in the same breath with Switzerland. Stranger things have come to pass, however, and the credentials of the prime minister of this Texas-sized country are worth examining—just in case a Switzerland-type caretaker should ever be needed out here in the Orient.

American diplomats trust U Nu because his record on communism is crystal clear—at least, insofar as it concerns the interior of Burma. Five years ago, when Burma was teetering on the rim of unmitigated disaster, U Nu saved the country from native Communists and assorted other rebels as surely as Abraham Lincoln saved the American union. Last December, U Nu visited Communist China and, out of humanitarianism, made a stirring plea for Prime Minister Chou En-lai to release eleven American fliers he had been holding for two years.

Also in Peiping, of all improbable places, U Nu delivered himself of a speech saying that he would like now to visit the

United States, whose people he praised as "brave and generous." An eyewitness describes the Red audience's reaction: "They absolutely froze in fear as his words came out. They were apparently torn between the need to applaud the pronouncements of a distinguished guest and the fear of being seen applauding." U Nu's comments undoubtedly contained the first kind words spoken about the United States inside China, at least in public, since the Communists booted Chiang Kai-shek off the mainland and across the Formosa Strait.

On the other hand, U Nu, in December 1949, became the first prime minister to recognize the Communist government of China, beating Nehru, of India, and Clement Attlee, of Great Britain, by a bunny's nose—although all three claim that "recognition" does not necessarily mean "endorsement." More recently, U Nu was a key figure among the five colored prime ministers who called the Asian-African conference . . . held in Indonesia [in April 1955]. To this unusual convocation he flatly refused to invite Chiang Kai-shek's anti-Communist Formosa government in addition to Chou En-lai's mainland government—although he was willing to admit both the Communists of North Vietnam (Vietminh) and the anti-Communists of South Vietnam.

During the same visit when he was telling the Peiping Communists nice things about the Americans, U Nu was buying a long line of Red goods. He came back to Rangoon saying, "The leaders of Communist China have a code of honor. They will not break a pledge, once given. In regard to Burma they have given a pledge of friendly relations, and I believe they will sincerely honor that pledge." This sounds like whistling in the dark by a man whose country shares more than a thousand miles of border with China—and has one fiftieth as many soldiers as China. The independent Rangoon newspaper, the *Nation,* observed, "It is something like saying to a dangerous animal, 'I know you are a good boy, and won't bite anyone,' when what one really means is, 'I hope you will be a good boy and not bite me.' "

His American friends were dismayed when U Nu ostentatiously smacked his lips after swallowing other Communist bait. He agreed to open air traffic between Burma and China, to exchange consulates and cultural missions—which the Communists have already exploited skillfully with sixty-seven of China's finest theatrical performers. With considerable naïveté U Nu accepted Chou En-lai's "categorical assurance" that the Chinese Communists had never even heard of the underground leader of the Burmese Reds, nor of other party leaders who recently crossed the border into China. Of course not!

One hot morning last October I called on U Nu at his home, a modest establishment which in British days housed the chairman of the Rangoon port commissioners. This was my first trip here since 1947. By design I had saved Burma as the last stop during a Far Eastern tour covering something over two years and more than a dozen countries. Prior to my October visit, Burma to me had been a memory of extreme violence— shortly after I left the last time the George Washington of that country, General Aung San, and most of his cabinet were wiped out in an orgy of assassination staged by a jealous politician named U Saw.

Paradoxically Burma was also a memory of shining countenances—half a century ago a young American mining engineer named Herbert Hoover tagged the Burmese as "the only truly happy and cheerful race in all Asia"—and of the calm that belongs to the deeply religious. It was the orgy of U Saw that had brought the reluctant young playwright U Nu—"a dreamer, a writer," he describes himself in one of his books—to the helm of the strife-ridden country.

When I saw him, U Nu was dressed, as usual, in Burmese attire—a *longyi* (saronglike skirt) of checkered pattern, a collarless shirt with gold buttons down the front, and a lightweight jacket like a pajama top with loops instead of buttonholes. On his head he wore the turbanlike *gaung baung,* a light, tight wicker basket fitted over by pink gauze tied in a knot behind the right temple. U Nu wore sandals, but no socks. Such a costume would draw stares in Kalamazoo; not so out here, where all men wear skirts and even the lowliest peasant owns one or two silk *longyi.* The prime minister's only concession to Western dress was a leather belt to hold up his *longyi;* most Burmese men simply twist the loose folds into a knot over the stomach, which gives them paunches they don't deserve.

U Nu entered the reception room, smiled engagingly and invited me to have a seat in an over-stuffed chair. The prime minister's English is excellent, though devoid of the Cantabrigian elegance which marks the speech of the British-educated Nehru. U Nu apologized because he could spare only half an hour, and asked if I cared to put some questions to him.

I wondered whether he had read an article in the London *Economist* which hinted that Burma might be the first of the "neutral" Asian nations to break away and join the American-sponsored SEATO, or Manila pact. No, he hadn't read this bit of speculation, but one of his ministers had told him about it. "Burma cannot join either of the blocs," he said politely but firmly; "we want to be friendly toward both sides."

One hears the same thing among all the neutrals. It seems to come more gracefully from this country of eighteen million than from big India, where the intellectuals try so hard to equate us American "capitalists" with the Chinese Communists that they wind up by concluding that nothing more is involved than a debate on economics—with, of course, the poor Chinese playing the underdog's role.

I understood the prime minister's position, I said, but suppose the Chinese repeated the Korean and Indo-Chinese pattern by arming the Communists already within the country?

"In that case we would change our attitude," said U Nu, but as an alert neutralist he quickly added, "—just as we would if the Anglo-American bloc started arming our enemies." To nail down his point he cited the case of a British correspondent who had come into Burma several years ago as the agent of a British colonel interested in arming Burma's Karen rebels, and had been caught with the incriminating documents in his Strand Hotel room. "We could have executed him, but we only put him in jail awhile and sent him out of the country because we didn't want to disrupt our relations with the British."

This interview took place not long after Chou En-lai had passed through Burma. There were reports that the Chinese prime minister had brandished a big stick during his conferences with the Burmese leader. "Oh, no, no, no," U Nu protested, "he just paid a friendly visit, like mine to China. You know, Chou En-lai seemed to me to be quite a liberal, not like other Communists—not like our own, who draw themselves up very stiff and look at you belligerently." . . .

At the . . . end [of World War II], the British saw the handwriting on the colonial wall and gave Burma back to the Burmese. They left behind a wretchedly unhealthy country where the infant mortality rate is 300 per 1000, but also the world's finest parliamentary system, an excellent judiciary and a surprising amount of good will, considering that the prime minister still speaks of the British time as "serfdom."

The Japanese [who had occupied the country in 1942-1945] made no friends in Burma, as U Nu emphatically testifies in his book on the occupation. But today the Japanese are drifting back. Last fall, U Nu's chief cabinet lieutenant, U Kyaw Nyein, negotiated the first Southeast Asian reparations pact with Japan, which must have such trade agreements to survive. Over ten years Japan has promised to pay $250 million in goods and services to Burma for World War II damages. In addition, Japanese contractors are building several Burmese Government factories as part of U Nu's eight-year plan of industrialization, modernization and socialization.

For one thing, Japan, which lacks 20 per cent of the food necessary to live, needs Burma's rice, although Formosan or Californian . . . rice pleases the palates of her citizens better. In an Asia which lacks enough to eat, Burma finds herself with a glut of rice—even though her export surplus amounts to only 1.5 million tons a year, about half the prewar figure. Burma has enough to eat all right—too much, in fact. U Nu floated a fancy trial balloon one day last fall when he suggested that the United States buy his 900,000 tons of surplus rice and give it to countries like India which can't afford to buy it. His balloon quickly flopped to earth, but he managed to get rid of 150,000 tons to Communist China, to be paid for 20 per cent in sterling,

50 per cent in goods from China and 30 per cent from Russia and Eastern Europe. To make this sale U Nu was willing to swallow Chou's bait.

Read the list of Asiatic nations receiving American economic aid this fiscal year, and you'll find nearly all the non-Communists there, from Afghanistan ($1.6 million) to South Korea ($280 million). But not Burma, which declined further aid two years ago—in fear of being identified with a "bloc," and in anger against the United States for aiding the Chinese Nationalist soldiers squatting on Burmese soil. Sometimes individual Burmese carry this independence to fantastic lengths—one of Rangoon's thirty-one daily newspapers (none has a circulation over 16,000) frequently lists a column unabashedly titled Read Soviet Books, but this paper inevitably prints a United States Information Service release on the same page.

Most of Burma's leaders got their political education in a hotbed of Marxism called the Rangoon University Student Union, but they contend it is the modern Communists who have let Marx down, whereas they themselves remain good non-Communist Marxists.

Burma's neutrals find in medal-bedecked Marshal Tito, of remote Yugoslavia, a kindred spirit. When he came to Rangoon last January he got the biggest reception ever accorded any visiting dignitary, including Chou En-lai, Admiral Arthur Radford, Jawaharlal Nehru and John Foster Dulles.

Yet one finds among the Burmese none of the sullen suspicion that marks the attitude of Indonesians and most Indians. Young Burmese, avid for knowledge of the modern world, literally devour the books and documentary films in the excellent USIS libraries of Rangoon and Mandalay; they laugh nervously at the yellow, hundred-cubicled Chinese Communist embassy behind its ten-foot-high enclosure and murmur, "The Great Wall has moved to Rangoon." One suspects that most knowledgeable Burmese have serious doubts about U Nu's declaration of faith in the Chinese "code of honor." Too many realize that, despite their prayers, their country's role may turn out to be not Switzerland but Czechoslovakia.

A FOOTHOLD FOR FREEDOM [8]

Aside from her gold-domed pagodas and Buddhist temples, the most popular place in all Burma is a simple American library which might have been whisked overnight on a magic carpet to Asia from any town or city between Maine and California. A huge, light-filled, book-lined room on the ground floor of a British bank in Rangoon, it radiates friendliness, informality and cheerful service in the best American tradition. Without fuss or fanfare, it has made thousands of friends for the United States in a part of the world where people automatically suspect and distrust the motives of the West and where the Communists' chief propaganda line is anti-Americanism.

Regarded by Washington as the most successful library the United States Information Agency has established anywhere abroad, it exemplifies the kind of aid which Asian countries really welcome. It benefits the community and is a part of it—and so is not an obvious device to sell a "bill of goods."

Every American who pays taxes for foreign aid can be proud of the way this United States institution has helped the young government of Burma—independent only since 1948—cope with Communist insurrection and build a stable country, probably the most hopeful one in Southeast Asia today. Since Burma's own Communists are in armed rebellion, since it shares a long border with a resurgent China which has historically been aggressive westward, and since a Peiping-directed Embassy in Rangoon actively conspires among the local Chinese community, Burmese leaders have not needed forced feeding of propaganda from Americans to understand and fight communism. What they have desperately needed—and what the American Library has consistently supplied—is information and help in setting up an administration and service so effective that the people would not become discontented and readily swallow the lies and promises of the Communists.

[8] From "A Model for U.S. Propaganda," article by Peggy Durdin, writer on Far Eastern affairs and wife of Tillman Durdin, chief correspondent of the New York *Times* in Southeast Asia. New York *Times Magazine*. p 13+. February 6, 1955. Reprinted by permission.

The library reaches not only officials but private citizens of all ages in every part of Burma. More than 1,300 Burmese come every day to this busy establishment. Men and women in gay sarongs pore over the racks of magazines, take notes from technical volumes, browse through the biography and fiction or, if they cannot read English, look at the brightly illustrated books in the children's annex. Pretty Burmese attendants decked with bits of glittering jewelry break with Asian custom by giving rich and poor, ragged and elegant, the same courteous attention. The patrons range from dirty little barefoot urchins, who sleep on the sidewalk at night, to dignified Buddhist monks and the highest officials of the Burmese Government.

The library's books travel by river boat, by plane and on the backs of human porters through and into Communist-held territory, across thousands of miles of jungle and mountains. Burmese read them eagerly in an umbrella cooperative in Bassein, a school in Mandalay, a prisoner's reading room in Myitkyina, an army officers' club in Akyab and a Youth League in Moulmein. A doctor who has to perform a complicated new operation, a merchant who wants to make "sparklers" and a landowner who plans to set up a model village on his property turn for help to the American library.

The father of a Communist university student borrowed a standard economics textbook, studied it and passed it on to his son. They discussed it together. When he returned the book the man said, "This book gave my son the true facts. He is no longer a Communist." . . .

The Burmese, official and civilian, appreciate the library because they so desperately needed it. . . . [After the war when] Burma got her independence . . . the country's future was jeopardized by large-scale armed rebellion, both Communist and non-Communist. . . . At the same time, the Burmese were faced with the tremendous tasks of rebuilding their badly damaged cities, roads and railways and setting up the entire machinery of government: central and local administrations, tax and education systems, public health, public works, police and defense forces. . . .

It was at this critical stage of Burma's development, when many of its friends wondered whether it would disintegrate into chaos, that the United States Information Agency appointed Zelma Graham to transform the little American reading room in Rangoon into a real library. A friendly, level-headed Pennsylvanian in her early forties, unmistakably and even typically American, the widow of a Baptist missionary in Burma, she had . . . worked for the American Army and government in India, North Burma, West China and Thailand. When she got the Rangoon job, she took a quick librarian's course at Columbia University and arrived in Burma when the country, like all newly independent, ex-colonial Asian nations, was full of suspicions and resentments of the West.

Mrs. Graham immediately inaugurated a lending service and began to harass Washington for books. She got them; she always gets them. She set up a few simple lines of policy, as American as pumpkin pie. First of all, she produced the first physically attractive library in all Burmese history; it has gay curtains, spacious tables, comfortable chairs and lots of space and light. The next great innovation was that books were placed on open shelves and everyone was encouraged to enjoy the hitherto unheard-of luxury of browsing through them.

Then she trained her staff of Americans, Burmese, Indians, Chinese and Pakistanis to disregard the demands of "face" and treat a shy, threadbare little clerk and the Chief Justice of Burma with exactly the same smiling courtesy. . . .

Perhaps most important of all, the library was and is designed, in solid American tradition, to be of service to the community and country, not as a propaganda device. When the sensitive and suspicious Burmese realized that propaganda was not going to be rammed down their throats, they began to throng to the American library. . . .

One important way in which the whole library contributes to Burmese-American friendship and indirectly counters Communist propaganda is that it gives the ordinary Burmese a chance to get acquainted, on his own initiative, with the real United States. Burmese ideas of America come chiefly from Communist literature and the poorer Hollywood movies.

As a result, they tend to think of the United States as a nation of selfish, wealthy, money-grubbers who cannot possibly understand or sympathize with the simple people and the problems of an underdeveloped Asian country. From the library's special exhibits, books and weekly educational films the Burmese build for themselves a much more accurate picture, one they accept because it has not been forced on them.

5. *Thailand*

FACTS ABOUT THAILAND [9]

Thailand literally means "Free Land." Formerly known as Siam, the country is almost the size of Texas, but compared to some of its huge neighbors in Asia, it is small.

Its major importance lies in its food production—rice, to be specific, and rice is the staple of diets in Asia and the Far East. Thailand is one of the few nations in this part of the world which has grown enough rice for itself and for sale, in important amounts, to hungry neighbors. Its rice exports annually have been between 1.4 and 1.6 million tons.

Almost all of Thailand's nineteen million people depend on the land for a living. Most live in small villages or in houses among their rice paddies. There is no land "problem" in the ordinary sense. Anybody can homestead a piece of ground which will assure him and his family at least a living.

In contrast to—and yet part of—Thailand's ruralism is its capital city of Bangkok. The capital bustles with more than a million people. And it constantly expands. Stores grow up around the city's edges, swallowing farms. A network of canals —which has earned Bangkok the name, "the Venice of the East" —enables the people to travel and move their goods by water as well as by road.

Bangkok's harbor opens into the Gulf of Siam, which is bordered by land rich with productive tin mines. And in the

[9] From *Thailand*, leaflet. (Country Series) Foreign Operations Administration. Washington, D.C. n.d.

interior of Thailand are iron, lignite, tungsten and other mineral deposits which are believed to be valuable and extensive.

Thailand's northeastern region—roughly one third of the nation—can be described as underdeveloped. A potentially rich farming area, it includes great stretches of arid land where irrigation dams now are being built. The irrigation program is one of the major projects on which the United States . . . is cooperating with the Thai Government, providing technical assistance and some dollar-financed equipment.

In this underdeveloped and underpopulated nation, which covers a little more than 200,000 square miles, there are few beggars. That is because the people are proud and, for a tropical country, energetic. Also, it is easy to grow one's food and catch fish; and shelter can be constructed out of bamboo and thatch. Furthermore, the year-round mild temperatures eliminate worry about fuel for heating and the need for warm clothes.

THAI POLITICS [10]

Thailand was the world's last important absolute monarchy. The king whose story was told in *Anna and the King of Siam* ruled as late as 1868, enjoying incredible power. His son, Chulalongkorn, also had the power of absolute life and death. His royal person was so sublime even in 1912 that no one could even think of touching him. He lost his first queen when she fell into a *klong* [canal], because no one present dared rescue her. (To do so would have required touching her sacred person.)

In 1932 the world was thrilled by the patriotic revolt of young officers educated in liberal Paris. In a bloodless coup they forced constitutional government upon the king, and modern Thailand was born. Unfortunately, the world's most curious government system was born at the same time. For in the succeeding twenty-two years there have been eleven major revolutions, five different constitutions and twenty changes of administration.

[10] From "Thailand—Jewel of Asia," article by James A. Michener, author of *Tales of the South Pacific* and other works, both fiction and nonfiction, dealing with Asia. *Reader's Digest.* 65:62-5. December 1954. Reprinted by permission.

A Thai revolution has no counterpart. Usually it consists of a brief bloodless battle between the army and the navy. In four of the principal revolutions no one was killed, and at one time the changes came so swiftly that they were irreverently dubbed "the annual Army-Navy game." The latest revolutions, however, have not been fun. In June 1951, many lives were lost, mostly civilians who were shot down in the crossfire.

No revolution has ever concerned any part of Thailand other than Bangkok. Three years after the first great revolt 70 per cent of Thailand was not even aware that a change in government had taken place. Today many back-country Thais have no idea who controls the government, aware only that young King Phumiphol (born in the United States) and his beautiful 23-year-old queen occupy the palace.

Power in Thailand is held by the Coup party, consisting of about four hundred veterans of the revolutions of 1932 and 1947. A revolution consists of a switch in power within this tight group, and being a Coup general is one of the best things that could happen to a man. Quickly you become a paid member of the boards of up to seventy important industries. Then you get some kind of semi-monopoly like matches, orange juice, mining tin or importing American automobiles. Of course, jobs are offered to all your family. It has been estimated that members of the Coup party and their relatives siphon off about 12 per cent of the national economy each year. The wealth of certain leaders is rumored to be incalculable. . . .

Today a new voice is heard in Thailand. It comes by radio from Communist China. It is the voice of a remarkable Thai, who once headed the government, calling on his people to embrace communism. Insiders who know Thailand say that only one thing could make Thailand go Communist: "Let the government foul up the rice market two more years." The ominous voice from China is sure that will happen.

Who is this ominous Thai who dreams of leading his people to communism? His record is almost unbelievable.

In 1932 the great democratic revolution was led by two handsome young men who had been studying and planning in Paris. Pibul was the effective organizer; Pridi, the brilliant theorist. Pibul was the dedicated soldier; Pridi, the ultra-sharp civilian. When their revolution succeeded, these two youngsters played major roles in forming the new government. They alternated as prime minister, worked hard to consolidate Thailand, grew rich together. They were the brains and the symbols of the new nation.

In 1941 these two young men faced ugly choices. Pibul, when Great Britain was unable to help Thailand, decided to back Japan. He declared war against the United States and led his nation into the mildest and most successful Japanese occupation during the war.

Pridi, on the other hand, decided that America was going to win, and he backed us to the hilt. At the risk of his own life he cooperated with our secret agents, forestalled the Japanese and paved the way for victory in Thailand. To most Americans Pridi became an established hero; Pibul, a proven rascal. Pridi had the support of the navy. Pibul was the darling of the army.

A bloody showdown came in 1949, and Pridi lost. This brilliant man, a rector of a large Thai university and champion of the people, went underground. His life was saved by American funds and it was rumored that he would someday soon again take over the government. Thousands of Thais longed for his return.

Now the switch has become complete. Pibul saw the menace of communism and led his government into what amounts to an alliance with the United States. He showed great courage in making this choice in favor of America, the nation against which he had once declared war. But he had the overwhelming support of the people of Thailand.

And last August Pridi, from Peiping, called upon the people of Thailand to revolt against the United States, the nation he had once risked his life to defend.

If the Thai Government were to wreck the rice market, if they were to oppress the citizens, and if Pridi were to offer vigorous leadership from just across the border, it is probable that Thailand would go Communist.

THE THREATS TO THAILAND [11]

The Communist threat which seems to worry Thailand, our SEATO [Southeast Asia Treaty Organization] ally in Southeast Asia, the most is the Thai Autonomous Republic which the Chinese have set up in the province of Yunnan. Thai leaders think this is intended as a base of operations for Pridi Phanomyong, former Thai Premier, who went over to the Communists and is now in China. American and British observers are skeptical. Although some Thai expatriates may be receiving Communist training there, they see little evidence that the Thai Autonomous Republic is actually being built up as an instrument of attack on Thailand, by either armed forces or large-scale subversion. They think the more instant threat to Thailand comes from northern Laos, which is under Communist control. At least one prominent Thai expatriate is in northern Laos with the rank of general. He has recruited some followers from Thailand and through his personal influence and old family connections, it is estimated that he might be able to muster the support of 250,000 to 500,000 Thais in northeast Thailand.

Also in northeast Thailand are some 50,000 Annamite refugees who want to go back to Communist North Vietnam but haven't been rounded up and moved yet. A fourth potential Communist threat lies in the 3.5 million Chinese who live in Thailand, but General Phao, chief of the Thai police, thinks this is not serious.

Defensive and counteroffensive measures are being taken against all four of these Communist threats. These include the building and improvement of roads to and along the northeast border of Thailand.

The Thai defenses against infiltration and subversion are not confined to Thailand, however. The Thais are reaching out to support their neighbors, especially Laos and Cambodia. Indo-China turns out to have been a purely artificial French creation. The natural affiliations of Laos and Cambodia are westward

[11] Article by Ernest K. Lindley, Washington columnist for *Newsweek*. *Newsweek*. 45:39. May 23, 1955. Reprinted by permission.

rather than with Vietnam, north or south. As a separate country, the landlocked splinter labeled Laos, with its some 1.5 million people, is an accident. The people of Laos and of northeast Thailand are of the same stock and have the same language. The most logical routes between Laos and the sea run through Thailand. These are being opened up to the economic and other benefit of Laos. If Laos survives as an independent state it will be due largely to support from and through Thailand. Sooner or later, it seems to this untutored observer, Laos should be federated or united with Thailand.

Cambodia has a different language, but cultural and religious ties with Thailand. Physical communications between the two countries are being restored and enlarged. Plans are well under way to develop a port through which Cambodia can be supplied, thus freeing her from her present dependence on Saigon.

Thailand and Burma recently buried their ancient enmity and have been exchanging good-will missions. Although Burma adheres to a policy of "noninvolvement" it has not criticized Thailand—or anyone else—for joining SEATO. Leading Thais have an understanding attitude toward Burma's neutrality. One of them said to me: "The heart of the Burmese is in the right place. You must not forget that they border China for more than a thousand miles." The Peiping radio has taken critical note of what it calls "the Buddhist bloc."

On its southern border, Thailand has been cooperating with Malaya in curbing the smuggling of arms and supplies to Communist guerrillas in Malaya. . . .

Thus there is much purposeful activity in and spreading out from Thailand. If the Thai defense base against communism, in the heartland of Southeast Asia, is not yet a rampart, neither is it a "paper tiger."

6. Indo-China

BASIC FACTS [12]

[Indo-China] comprises a group of three Associated States of the French Union—Vietnam, Laos and Cambodia. . . . Indo-

[12] From "The A.B.C.'s of Indo-China." New York *Times.* p E5. April 11, 1954. Reprinted by permission.

China forms the long Pacific flank of Southeast Asia—bounded on the north by Communist China and on the west by vulnerable Burma and Thailand. The area of Indo-China is 286,000 square miles, one-third larger than France. It is a rugged, tropical country with a mountainous terrain.

Of Indo-China's population of 28 million, 80 per cent live in Vietnam. The population is clustered most heavily in the delta areas, where density is about 1,550 per square mile (twice that of Rhode Island). . . .

The predominant ethnic group is the Annamese, a simple people of Chinese origin, who have, however, thrown off the yoke of Chinese rule several times in their long history. On their Buddhist traditions have been implanted the cultural influences of the French, who number only about fifty thousand. The country has a well-established system of French and native schools.

Indo-China is predominantly agricultural and is a main source of supply for the basic food staple of the Far East—rice—which constitutes 25 per cent of Indo-Chinese exports. Over the years, billions of dollars have been profitably invested by the French in Indo-China's plantations; in mines to develop its mineral resources (coal, zinc, tin, iron); in processing plants, in road and rail communications. Indo-China is part of the raw material-rich complex of Southeast Asia .. . . But the standard of living remains one of the world's lowest: Food supply per capita is just about 2,000 calories a day (among major countries, only India and Burma are below that), and per capita income is less than $100 a year.

Vietnam, Cambodia and Laos, former colonies of the old French Empire, have held since 1949 their present status within the French Union—the federal organization that includes the French Republic, its Associated States and Associated Territories. As Associated States, the three Indo-China countries are technically independent in domestic affairs and coordinate with France in foreign affairs. Each state has its own courts, its own civil service and parliamentary government. Each has its own national army. However, France maintains troops and bases in Indo-China and has a determining influence on trade and currency matters. International affairs are shaped by the Council of the French Union in Paris, in which each of the Associated States is represented, but in which French Foreign Office policy is dominant. There is, in all three of the states, considerable agitation for the removal of these French limitations on complete independence.

[France's war in Indo-China began in 1946 when negotiations with the Vietminh movement—led by Ho Chi Minh, a Moscow-trained revolutionary—broke down and Vietminh guerrillas attacked French installations. It went on for eight years, and was finally halted by a cease-fire agreed upon at the Geneva conference on Far Eastern problems of 1954. Under the terms of the settlement the French surrendered all of Vietnam north of the seventeenth parallel, an area of 77,000 square miles with a population of about twelve million, to the Vietminh. The Communists agreed to evacuate their guerrillas from south Vietnam and Cambodia. They also agreed to evacuate all of Laos except for two northern provinces. According to the agreement, both north and south Vietnam are to consult and hold elections for an all-Vietnam government not later than July 26, 1956.—Ed.]

DIVIDED VIETNAM [13]

[The 1954] Geneva conference resulted in the creation, at least temporarily, of two countries in Vietnam. This elongated tropical land became the third nation, after Germany and Korea, to be divided by the struggle between world Communist and anti-Communist forces.

The process of splitting Vietnam into a Communist north and a non-Communist south was completed only [in May 1955] as the last French Union troops evacuated from above, and the last acknowledged Vietminh forces transferred from below, the seventeenth parallel. Since then the two Vietnam governments have operated with full sovereignty in their respective territories

[13] From "Divided Vietnam—Comparison After One Year," news story by Tillman Durdin, chief New York *Times* correspondent in Southeast Asia. New York *Times*. p E4. July 17, 1955. Reprinted by permission.

and their separate characteristics and potentialities have been more sharply manifested.

Here is the way the two Vietnams—the Democratic Republic of Vietnam in the north and the State of Vietnam in the south—compare:

The Geneva settlement gave the north slightly less territory but more population than the south. No reliable census has been taken in Vietnam for decades. Estimates vary, but the population figures of 13 million for the north and 10 million for the south are generally accepted here [in Saigon].

The Vietnamese of the north are regarded as being more energetic than those of the south. Both territories have big river delta rice bowls, but the north is overpopulated and some years does not grow enough food for its people. The south is less crowded and has a food surplus.

The north is more rural than the south. In bustling Saigon, with its more than two million population, the south has one of the great modern cities of Asia. There are a number of other cities of more than 100,000 population in the south, and below the seventeenth parallel is Hue, Vietnam's ancient dynastic capital, built a century and a half ago as a small-scale replica of Peiping.

The north's biggest city is tree-shaded Hanoi with its 300,000 population. The ports of Haiphong and Vinh have half as many residents, but aside from these three, the north has no other centers worthy of being called cities.

Undoubtedly the north is politically stronger at the moment than the south. The government of the Democratic Republic of Vietnam is an authoritarian regime dominated by the Vietnamese Communist party (called the Laodang or Labor party). There are nationalist non-Communists in the north Vietnam government, which is officially called a coalition responsible to an assembly elected nearly ten years ago, but the non-Communists have little power.

The government under President Ho Chi Minh is proceeding with the establishment of a typical Communist system in the north. Lands are being redistributed to the accompaniment of people's court trials, imprisonment, controls on economic activities, and all private enterprise except small-scale business and farming is being eliminated.

While there is forced labor and detention for political opponents of the northern government, the republic has not gone in for large-scale liquidations, and the regime so far is milder than the Communist government of neighboring China.

In the south Premier Ngo Dinh Diem still has a considerable distance to go before his government can claim to have consolidated the unity of its area and establish itself on a stable political basis. The government is still in the process of suppressing two rebellious groups. Other lesser armed opposition bands remain to be dealt with, and effective administrative control in some regions is still lacking.

Premier Diem and his government have gained steadily in effectiveness and popularity since he took the leadership of south Vietnam . . . [in 1954]. Its organized political backing is still unstable, however, and a network of Vietminh agents, working in the interests of the north, still has widespread influence, particularly among the peasantry.

The north has reorganized its armed forces and increased their effectiveness since the armistice. It is estimated that the Vietminh regime has some 150,000 well-armed men in first line regiments and divisions and possibly another 150,000 auxiliaries of various kinds.

The south has an army of about 180,000 men plus a constabulary and other armed units totaling approximately another 50,000. The south is demobilizing and aims now at a permanent army of 150,000 men. The south already has a small air force and navy—branches which the north does not possess— and is engaged in building these services up into striking forces of real power.

The troops of the south are more mechanized and better armed than those of the north but at the moment the north— largely because of the more extensive training and combat experience of its forces—is stronger militarily than the south.

The south is economically better off at present than the north and potentially stronger. With its surplus production of rice and other foods, the south is able to feed its people. By contrast the north had bad crops last year and famine conditions have prevailed in some districts.

At present the Communist republic of the north is the stronger of the two Vietnams. Political unity, a larger and more energetic population, better military forces and tough singleness of purpose weigh in favor of the north. The north's Communist network in the south, plus the continued existence of a considerable amount of pro-Vietminh sentiment among the southerners, also count in measuring up the north's total national position.

At present the north would win national elections if they were held and would also win a military conflict if the two Vietnams went to war unaided on either side by outside forces.

With time the balance could swing in favor of the south. If political unity is achieved, and social, military, economic and administrative programs now under way are realized, the south could overhaul the north's advantages. A free, stable and democratic system in the south could be the most positive and effective force of all in undermining the Communist hold on the people of the north and eliminating Communist influence in the south.

NGO DINH DIEM OF VIETNAM [14]

Premier Ngo Dinh Diem, a resilient, deeply religious Vietnamese nationalist, . . . is burdened with the terrible but challenging task of leading the 10.5 million people of south Vietnam from the brink of communism into their long-sought state of sovereign independence. No man in troubled Asia is confronted by more obstacles on the road to order and justice. [Three religious-political sects—Cao Dai, Hoa Hao and Binh Xuyen, the last under the leadership of bandits and river pirates—control the southern portion of south Vietnam and threaten his life.] The refugees from the Communist half of Vietnam, now exceeding 500,000 and still pouring south at the rate of 10,000 a week, are pleading for food, housing and jobs. In-

[14] From "South Vietnam, the Beleaguered Man," article. *Time.* 65:22-5. April 4, 1955. Courtesy *Time* Magazine; copyright Time Inc. 1955.

experience—his own and his people's—make leaders hard to find, ideas scarce, and decisions difficult to make. ("This government," said one of the United States officials anxiously trying to help, "is stuck together by Scotch tape, bits of string and putty.") The French, striving to maintain by fair means and by sly means a remnant of influence and profit in the land they have exploited for seven decades, obstruct him with the wily rearguard maneuvers of colonialism.

But, above all, Diem's enemy is a coalition of Communists and the calendar. With no personal political organization, a civil service that is amateur and an army still in training, the Premier of south Vietnam is charged with building a government and a popularity strong enough to overcome the strength and skill of Ho Chi Minh's Communist regime in North Vietnam. Under the Geneva pact, which sliced the country in two, the south Vietnamese have only [until July 1956] to prepare to meet Ho's Communists in a nation-wide test at the polls, winner take all. . . .

Ngo Dinh Diem seems at first glance an improbable man for a fight against Ho Chi Minh, the wispy, twisting, one-time chef's assistant who is so resolutely Communist, yet so clever that much of Asia still toys with the notion that he is really just a Vietnamese patriot. Diem's career has grown mostly out of negative decisions. He is a sparsely gifted administrator, and of politics he says: "Clever maneuvers only betray, demoralize, and divide the people." To some of the more sophisticated in the game, he rates as a marginal man.

Yet such is Vietnam, disgusted with colonialism and its vices, frustrated in its yearning for freedom, that a leader's integrity is more important than his ability. Communist Ho has built popular support not altogether with wiliness and Communist doctrine, but also with incorruptibility and his undeviating enmity for French colonial rule. Ngo Dinh Diem brings into the battle an incorruptibility even greater and his own record of a lifetime's opposition to French rule and influence. "There are only two real leaders in Vietnam," Ho's chief of staff, General Vo Nguyen Giap, recognized some time ago. "One is Ho Chi Minh. The other is Ngo Dinh Diem. There is no room in the country for both."

Diem is a stocky (5 ft. 4 in., 143 lbs.), young-looking man of 54, with thick black hair and a penchant for white Western-style sharkskin suits. His eyes peer out distantly from beneath heavy lids. He is a lonely man, unused to self-expression, who lets others bring up the subject and then blurts, interminably and at random, not always expressively. . . . Though Diem was born in a straw hut on his father's estate near Hue (where his ailing, eighty-seven-year-old mother still lives behind a wall to keep off evil spirits), he is of the upper class, and he talks without self-consciousness of "the little people." He is proud of his Vietnamese heritage: "We are a country of principles, an old country, a country built village by village. Vietnam is a solid thing. . . ."

Ngo Dinh Diem comes from a clan of leaders who for a thousand years defended the Vietnamese against invaders from China. In the seventeenth century, the Ngo Dinh clan was converted to Roman Catholicism. . . . (Today Vietnam, essentially Buddhist, has about two million Catholics.)

Ngo Dinh Diem's father, . . . was a mandarin first class at the court of the old emperor, wearing the traditional silken robes and two-inch fingernails. . . . [He] was also one of Vietnam's foremost educators, and his nine children got the benefit of it. . . . At fifteen, Ngo Dinh Diem took the first of his big negative decisions: having begun training for the priesthood, he decided after a few weeks not to go through with it. At seventeen he took his second: he decided not to go to college in France. "Those of us who did go to France came back a mixture of many things," . . . [a] brother said, "but Diem is pure Vietnamese." At twenty Diem graduated top of his class from the French-run civil service school at Hanoi, soon made his way up to district chief, administrator of 225 villages. . . . In 1929, at 28, he became a provincial governor; at 32 he became Minister of the Interior in the puppet government of the French. Three months later, he demanded more independence. The French would not give it. Diem resigned.

Diem spent the next seven years in passive resistance to the French exploitation of his country. . . .

During World War II and its aftermath, the Japanese, the French and Ho Chi Minh's Communists all fought one another for Indo-China; all three wanted support from Nationalist Diem but he refused them all because none of them stood for "true independence."

In 1945, Ho's Communist troops struck at the nationalist Ngo Dinh clan, raiding the mansion at Hue and burning Diem's collection of ten thousand books. The Communists arrested Diem; they . . . [killed] Diem's respected elder brother, Ngo Dinh Khoi. . . . [Diem was freed about four months later by Ho.—Ed.]

In December 1946, when Ho and the French broke into the Indo-China war, Diem proclaimed himself against both sides. In April 1947 he started his first positive, political movement, a third-force, nonviolent outfit called the "National Union Front." The French promptly banned it. Three years later Ngo Dinh Diem turned to the outside for friends of Vietnamese independence, and took off for Europe and the United States. For the best part of two years (1951-1953) he made his home at the Maryknoll Junior Seminary in Lakewood, New Jersey, often going down to Washington to buttonhole State Department men and congressmen and urge them not to support French colonialism. "The French may be fighting the Communists," Diem argued, "but they are also fighting the people." . . .

[During the decisive battle when the Communists captured Dienbienphu in May 1954] Diem discerned that his time to serve might be at hand. . . . The French, in part because they needed someone on whom to unload catastrophe, offered Diem the Vietnam premiership, with their first acceptable promise of independence. On June 15, 1954, Ngo Dinh Diem took the job and headed back to Saigon. "We don't know where we're going," said one of his aides, contemplating chaos, "but the captain is reliable and our boat is clean."

Diem's record of nationalist purity did not, at first, get Premier Diem very far. France's Premier Mendès-France was advocating "concessions . . . large concessions" to end the war, and at Geneva he made them. "We weren't even consulted," complained Diem's Foreign Minister Tran Van Do. Back in

Saigon, Diem found that he could not depend on a single Vietnamese battalion; he had nothing in the treasury; he could not make contact with about 85 per cent of his villages. Hundreds of thousands of refugees were coming down from the Communist north, choosing freedom, however chaotic, and needing care.

Diem's first crisis came from the headquarters of General Nguyen Van Hinh, flamboyant, pro-French commander of the Vietnamese army. General Hinh tried to edge into power by edging his 200,000 men into a gradual, nonviolent kind of mutiny. Diem was cool, but with the resources at his command he could not cope with Hinh. But through United States influence, he finally won. "I had only to lift my telephone," the general explained, "and the *coup d'état* was on. But I was told that if it happened, the Americans would cut off all dollar aid."

Diem's victory put General Hinh into exile and his nationalists into forward motion. Those who had waited to see who would win, now began to move over toward the Premier. United States aid and advice began to take hold. . . .

Never very close to the people, Diem set out on a grass-roots tour of central Vietnam and got a welcome that astonished his advisers. "Long live Ngo Dinh Diem!" the people cheered. "I've seen so-called 'spontaneous demonstrations' all over Asia," said an American after one demonstration, "but this was different . . . Fifteen thousand people came charging across the field toward him, screaming, waving straw hats, like the stampede in *King Solomon's Mines*."

Encouraging as they are, Diem's accomplishments are minor compared to what remains to be done in attaining law and order and building public confidence. Stubborn and negative-minded, Diem disquiets some of his countrymen by his continued withdrawal, and by his tendency to lean for advice more on three of his brothers, Bishop Ngo Dinh Thuc, Ngo Dinh Luyen and Ngo Dinh Nhu, than on his Cabinet. His reluctance to delegate authority has led him to fantastic time-consuming pettiness. Samples: recently he took over himself the granting of all entry and exit visas and the scrutiny of all currency exchange applications. But the United States military, diplomatic and technical experts, while noting the shortcomings, have not let them dull the conviction that Diem is Vietnam's soundest hope. "After some doubts about Premier Diem," said one high United States official, "I think that they have been resolved in his favor and that he is entitled to full and unqualified support."

An Asian tradition has it that if one saves a man's life, one is thenceforth responsible for his destiny. The United States in a sense is lumping those two missions into one simultaneous undertaking in south Vietnam. In addition to its millions and its prestige, Washington invested the talents of a thousand Americans in the country, with the ex-Army chief of staff, General J. Lawton Collins, as the top United States emissary. Among them: for land reform, Wolf Ladejinsky, the celebrated Agriculture Department expert who did the land reform job in postwar Japan; for maneuvering against the Communists, Colonel Edward Lansdale, the officer who played such a helpful role in the rise of Philippines President Ramon Magsaysay that Filipinos gave him a post-election title of "General Landslide."

The Americans are finding Premier Diem increasingly receptive to advice and ideas, and by no means a puppet. He refuses to be pushed or rushed. . . . Out of the occasional buckings and tight moments has come a partnership that shows progress and promises more. Premier Diem admires Americans because "they don't lie."

LAOS AND CAMBODIA [15]

The future of the two Buddhist monarchies of Laos and Cambodia is much brighter, by contrast, [than that of Vietnam], barring outright aggression from the Vietminh or China. Throughout the civil war the Vietminh always concentrated its primary efforts in Vietnam. Although both Laos and Cambodia were eventually invaded, operations in these countries were es-

[15] From *New Nations of Southeast Asia*, pamphlet by William Henderson, research associate at the Council on Foreign Relations. (Headline Series no 110) Foreign Policy Association. New York. March-April 1955. p52. Reprinted by permission.

sentially side shows. Since Geneva the Communists have evacuated their forces, except from a part of Laos bordering on north Vietnam, where a dissident Laotian government continues to function.

In neither country is the legacy of civil war likely to constitute a severe handicap to progress. The rebel movements never had much support among the devout Buddhist populations of Laos and Cambodia. To be sure, inefficiency and corruption are also found here, as well as extreme political immaturity, illiteracy and poverty. But neither country has to face anything like the problems confronting south Vietnam, and both possess the inestimable advantage of governments popular with their peoples.

It is true that the constitutional regimes inaugurated in both countries in 1947 are likely to remain façades hiding the reality of autocratic rule, but in the absence of any demand for democratic government this may not prove too serious. . . . If the Communists should eventually win all of Vietnam, however, the position of Laos and Cambodia would soon become precarious.

7. Malaya

THE "EMERGENCY" [16]

In Malaya . . . the military threat of communism has been reduced, if not yet entirely eliminated. A well-equipped British army of about forty thousand men is gradually whittling down Communist terrorists and slowly widening the so-called "white" (cleared of Reds) areas. . . .

The guerrillas are real Communists, although the British authorities, for psychological-political reasons, refuse to identify them as such. The British refer to them as "terrorists" in order to minimize their political appeal. To call them by the true name of Communist, the British feel, might add to their prestige

[16] From "Burma and Malaya: Jungle War Against Communism," article by Saul K. Padover, dean of the School of Politics, New School for Social Research. *Foreign Policy Bulletin.* 33:6-7. August 1, 1954. Reprinted by permission.

among the Chinese communities in Malaya, particularly since these latter communities contain an indeterminate number of sympathizers with Red China.

Virtually all the Malay terrorists, perhaps as many as 99 per cent, are Chinese. This is perhaps the most significant aspect of the conflict. Malaya, it should be kept in mind, is made up of three racial communities. Of the ten million inhabitants in Malaya, about five million are Chinese, around four million are Malay, and approximately one million are Tamil Indians. The British, who had largely settled and organized modern Malaya, had traditionally favored the Malay race at the expense of the numerically larger Chinese community. This is one of the basic causes of the troubles in Malaya today.

The Chinese complain that the British had always been unfriendly to them. They point out that they always had to support their own schools, while the Malay schools were maintained by the British at public expense. The Chinese have long felt galled at being discriminated against in the matter of jobs, especially in the civil service. Many a young Chinese has been convinced that so long as the British remain in power he had no future in Malaya. It is these embittered young people who, under Communist leadership and inspiration (there are about five hundred fanatical Red leaders), have taken to the jungle to fight against the British. They have had active or tacit support from many Chinese villages, although nowadays in steadily decreasing numbers.

The British reply to the Chinese accusations is that the Malays are a nonbusiness-minded, easy-going people who are no match for the Chinese in any competitive effort. They need protection from the energetic, enterprising, practical-minded Chinese, who own and control most of Malaya's small-scale businesses (big enterprises are still in European hands). Malaya's Chinese also own 20 per cent of the rubber industry and 25 per cent of the tin mines. The Malays, on the other hand, are almost completely out of the business and financial picture. The bulk of them make their living on the land. Left unprotected, the British say, the Malay people would become the subjects of the economically powerful and ambitious Chinese. Consequently, Britain has considered it a duty to favor the weaker against the stronger. The British have fostered education among the Malay people and have encouraged them to enter government service. Although the Chinese are nowadays no longer barred from offices or jobs, it is true, nevertheless, that the majority of Malaya's police and civil service consists of Malays.

This British policy, which the Chinese have branded as "Divide and rule," has led to the present conflict in Malaya. It is probably true that the great majority of Chinese in Malaya, particularly in such old British settlements as Penang, Malacca and Singapore, are anti-Communists and in favor of continued British occupation, provided they are given a large measure of self-government. Still, a minority of the Chinese have shown themselves either friendly to communism, especially to Red China, or hostile to the British. This group has given secret support and encouragement to the Red terrorists in the jungle.

The war in Malaya is now in its eighth year and shows no signs of ending in the foreseeable future. Although on a relatively small scale, the conflict there has been both sanguinary and costly. . . . There is no doubt that the British forces are slowly winning the struggle. But it will still take much time, persistence, military effort and bloodshed before Malaya is free of Communist terrorism. In the meantime, the British are wisely pursuing a double policy in that rich colony. On the one hand, they are waging an intelligently conducted military war against the terrorists. On the other hand, and simultaneously, they are helping to create a genuine Malay nationality. They have set up a governing council, which contains representatives of the three major communities. They are encouraging self-government and democratic procedures on local levels. They have extended Malay citizenship to non-Malays, especially Chinese. In Singapore they have been friendly to the formation of political parties on non-racial lines. Throughout the peninsula there are now developing democratic trade unions that are open to members of all three races. . . .

In sum, the British—and the free world—are generally meeting with success in Malaya. Some day, when the Red threat has been ended and the Malayan inhabitants have shown ability

to rule themselves democratically, as they are now beginning to
do, Britain will feel free to grant Malaya full independence. It
is the conviction that Britain will do this in the not very distant
future which stimulates the majority of Malaya's diverse people
to support the British in their war against communism.

8. *Indonesia*

INDONESIA'S COMMUNISTS [17]

In the fluid, casual atmosphere of Indonesia, accumulating
solid, clear-edged facts resembles reaching for eels. But one
can at least dispose of some of the lurid misconceptions about
these islands which are current abroad.

Indonesia is not catastrophically disintegrating. It is not
teetering dizzily on the edge of the Communist precipice. The
PKI (Partei Komunis Indonesia) is far from the point of
power and influence where Mao's party in China or Ho's followers in Indo-China stood in 1948. Indonesia's magnetic President Sukarno is no Communist. Neither is the suave and
handsome [former] Prime Minister, Dr. Ali Sastroamidjojo,
nor the members of his Cabinet, although several are Marxists
and sympathetic to the Communists.

[Dr. Ali Sastroamidjojo's government, formed in 1953, re-
lied on Communist votes to remain in power in the latter part
of its period in office. This cabinet fell, however, in July 1955
and was succeeded by a twelve-party coalition—without Communist participation or support—pending the outcome of elections which began at the end of September 1955 and lasted more
than a month. Preliminary results showed the Partei Nasional
Indonesia (PNI)—the nationalists led by Dr. Sastroamidjojo—
leading. Next largest was the Masjumi, or Moslem party. Third
was another Moslem party, Nahdatal Ulama, and fourth in
strength was the Communist party.—Ed.]

[17] From "Analysis of Communism in Indonesia," article by Peggy Durdin,
writer on Far Eastern affairs and wife of Tillman Durdin, chief correspondent of
the New York *Times* in Southeast Asia. New York *Times Magazine.* p 13+.
March 13. 1955. Reprinted by permission.

But many thoughtful Indonesians and a number of the country's foreign friends are worried over the Communists' recent rate of growth and their potential. Indonesia is like a garden where a hardy weed, formerly under control, has really begun to thrive for the first time.

A few years ago the Communists were in the parliamentary opposition, isolated, in half-disrepute, operating very quietly and cautiously under the eye of the police. Today . . . they work openly and vigorously. They have managed to infiltrate some men into the government.

Their goal is a rich prize, for there is a good deal to win in Indonesia. Its wealth and its location north of the British Commonwealth country of Australia and south of the dollar-producing British colony of Malaya mean it has considerable economic and strategic interest for Peiping and Moscow. This great chain of tropical islands straddling the Equator is potentially the richest country east of India and south of China, with large natural resources and sizable exports of tin, rubber, copra, oil, tea and spices.

Indonesia's population is half that of the United States, scattered over a thousand islands of all shapes and sizes, the smallest just a dot of shining sand circled by lively colored fish and decorated with a palm tree, the largest bigger than California. Green, lush and sun-warmed, patterned with oblong rice fields which reflect straight palms, bamboo, cone-shaped volcanic mountains, and white clouds sailing through a bright blue sky, the islands each vary from one another somewhat in terrain and culture.

There are, for instance, oil and rubber-rich Sumatra, where tigers roam through a central spine of jungle; the spice islands of the Moluccas; Madura, famous for its salt production and its yearly bull races; little Bali, where to dance, carve, weave and paint beautifully are still functions of everyday life; Banka, the tin producer, and Java, where the great Buddhist monument of Borabudur calls up the past and the republic's bustling capital, Jakarta, looks to the future.

Living in simple, sometimes primitive fashion on the Indonesian islands are a small-boned, slight, handsome, brown-skinned people who move with grace. Though capable of violence, they are generally courteous, soft-voiced, hospitable and quick to smile or laugh. Most of them are little farmers; more than half cannot read or write. The great majority are Moslems, bearing, however, very strong traces of the country's early Hindu period and even remoter animist past.

Perhaps because the air is soft and warm and the earth rich and generous, life for Indonesians has far less sense of pressure and urgency than for people living on niggardly soil in colder climates. Time itself loses significance where rice can be grown the whole year round, day fades gently into night, and one season is almost indistinguishable from the next.

It is in this atmosphere that a young Indonesian Republic has been trying to establish solid democratic institutions. It has had full independence for only five years, after more than two centuries of Dutch rule. Largely because of Dutch colonial policy, its administrative machinery is still inadequate and inefficient. The country's industry and commerce remain chiefly in foreign hands, Dutch and Chinese. Links between the capital and some of the outer islands are often tenuous and four or five local rebellions persist like stubborn abscesses. . . .

The . . . major political parties in Indonesia are . . . the Masjumi or Moslem party, the PNI (Partei Nasional Indonesia), the Communists and the Socialists.

The Masjumi is [important] . . . because, in this Moslem country, its chief plank is the establishment of a state based on Koranic principles. [Another Moslem party, the Nahdatal Ulama, or Moslem Scholar's party, also has a strong popular following— Ed.] The PNI is an ultra-nationalist party including all shades of political opinion, from a pro-Communist left wing to a very conservative right wing. (Although he is technically outside politics, this is the party which Sukarno in fact supports.) The Socialists have a very limited following which includes some of the country's best talent and intelligence. Both the Socialists and the Masjumi are strongly and actively anti-Communist. . . .

Westerners can better understand the PNI's relaxed attitude toward the Communists if they remind themselves that (1)

Marxism was practically required reading for Indonesian nation-alists all through the twenties and thirties; (2) even the Asians who reject communism today do not view it with the horrified repugnance characteristic of the average American's attitude; and (3) the Communists are one of Indonesia's oldest political parties, made respectable—except for one memorable occasion— by their thirty-year-long support of national independence. . . .

The Communists worked with the nationalist underground against the Japanese during the war and reorganized openly in 1946. At first they cooperated with the Indonesian nationalists in their bitter war for independence against the Dutch. But when Moscow gave the word in 1948 for Asian Communists to bid openly for power, the PKI . . . rebelled . . . against the republican government of President Sukarno, which was fighting the Dutch. This insurrection—famous, or rather, infamous in Indonesian history under the title of the Madiun Affair—was totally suppressed by the Indonesian Government and Com-munist leaders who could not melt away to China or Russia were executed.

The Madiun Affair was near-fatal for the PKI. It was politi-cal sacrilege: armed rebellion against a revolutionary Indonesian Government fighting a sacred war for the country's independ-ence. It put the Indonesian Communists under a cloud of dis-grace from which they are only now emerging. . . .

For the moment . . . the Communists are working to lull any existing Indonesian fears of Communist China, convert the country to an uncritical, all-guards-down acceptance of coexist-ence, increase trade and other ties between Indonesia and the Communist bloc and—perhaps first priority—fan to the utmost the anti-American sentiment already in existence. . . .

The Communists themselves say openly that they have made great progress in the last year. The government's policies, they say, "give every chance of development to people's organizations, the Communist party and other democratic parties." From a membership around seven thousand a few years ago, the Com-munists now claim 500,000 members and candidates (still far less than the PNI or Masjumi). Their para-military organization of ex-guerrillas has about 200,000 members. There are thousands more in their trade unions and peasants' organizations. . . .

The Communists continue to dominate the Indonesian labor movement, as they have done for decades. SOBSI, the labor federation they control, could stop the railroads, shipping and the production of tin and rubber next week if it wished. The Communists refrain from big spectacular labor conflicts these days but they stage constant sitdowns and slowdowns against foreign-owned concerns.

Many Communist labor organizers are diverting their attention to the Indonesian peasant. . . . But no one in Indonesia seems to know just how successful the Communists are with the great mass of Indonesian farmers, whose lives are focused around their little rice fields, their water buffalo, their lively children, their palm-thatched huts, the occasional festival, the ever-present, unseen world of animist spirits and their Moslem faith.

The Moslem religion is in fact the chief weapon the Masjumi is using against the Communists in the Indonesian countryside. It doesn't always work. . . . A wealthy Indonesian of Chinese ancestry was chatting one day in her car with a chauffeur who had been with various branches of her family for twenty years and who read regularly the anti-Communist newspapers to which she subscribed.

"How are you going to vote in the elections this year?" she asked.

"I'm going to vote PKI," he said.

"Why?" she asked.

"Because when the Communists come to power," he said, "everyone will have nice houses like yours. And all the land and property of the rich will belong to the common people."

"But how can you believe in the Communists? I thought you were a good Moslem," she said.

The chauffeur laughed. "Oh, the Masjumi is all right for religion," he said, "but the Communists are the people for improving our everyday life."

Perhaps first among the factors working for the Communists is the organization and discipline of the PKI, markedly superior to that of the other political parties. PKI leaders are young (only in their early thirties) but they are devout and energetic. They have behind them older, more experienced, Moscow-oriented party members, as well as the benefit of advice from Dutch, Chinese and Russian Communists (the last two well represented in Jakarta embassies).

Moreover the PKI has plenty of money, in spite of its very low-income membership. Only the Communists can afford to pay workers right down to the village level, put out a steady flow of propaganda literature and send Indonesians for training and visits abroad. . . .

But there are important factors working against the Indonesian Communists. They are especially plain to anyone who watched the Communists take China and half Vietnam as termites patiently destroy a building.

First of all, the PKI has, at present, no "Yenan" (secure politico-military base) and no real army. The Indonesian army and police force are anti-Communist.

Secondly, unlike the Vietminh, the PKI cannot use the fight for national independence as a rallying cry, except in the economic field—and Irian. (If the Dutch really want to hurt Indonesian communism, they should simply give New Guinea to Indonesia.)

Thirdly, there are in Indonesia—as there were not in China—many highly intelligent people among the middle class and the intelligentsia, in and outside government, who really believe in the possibility of achieving a workable form of democracy and are very sophisticated about the real nature of communism.

Fourthly, there is little real misery and hopeless poverty on which Communists can capitalize. The price of Indonesia's staple food, rice, is steady.

Lastly, although government in Indonesia is very inefficient and increasingly corrupt, it is by no means generally discredited, as was the Kuomintang in China.

The Indonesian Government has made remarkable progress in the field of both child and adult education. The country's two universities are slowly solving such mammoth problems as changing the language of instruction from Dutch to English and

Indonesian. All over Indonesia there are idealistic and conscientious officials, unknown and unsung, who are working hard and getting jobs done. More and more farmers are trying improved agricultural methods and joining cooperatives. . . .

The Indonesian Communists cannot hope to achieve control of Indonesia in the immediate future. They can . . . win a sizable number of parliamentary seats. . . . Perhaps they may be able slowly to continue to infiltrate party members or fellow-travelers into the administration and place some of their men in the police and army. They can reach a widening number of workers, peasants and young people. Through front organizations and membership on semi-official committees, they will propagate sugar-coated versions of their main ideas.

But these actions generate reaction. It is possible that the PKI has overplayed its hand in Indonesia. What Communist activity may produce in the end is a healthy coalition of all the country's anti-Communist groups, working to evolve a sound, Asian-type democracy which will bring a better life to the Indonesian people.

INDONESIA'S FOREIGN POLICY [18]

Indonesia's foreign policy of active neutralism is so firmly rooted in the experiences of her colonial past that there is little likelihood that the country will, in the foreseeable future, become a part of the free world bloc.

In the Indonesian mind the threat in the "cold war" comes from neither the Communist nor the free world side. It comes rather from any nation on either side that has colonial designs.

It is an unfortunate circumstance that, in the thinking of the Indonesians, the members of the Western bloc have been traditionally a part of the colonial pattern.

There is, therefore, a basic suspicion of the motivation of the West.

[18] From "Indonesia Backs Neutralist Aims," news story by Robert Alden, New York *Times* Southeast Asia correspondent. New York *Times*. p8 June 7, 1955. Reprinted by permission.

When the United States offers the Indonesian Republic aid that goes beyond technical assistance, the government—and a large number of people as well—feels there is danger that colonialism, routed politically in Indonesia, is trying to return through economic infiltration.

The delicate matter of sovereignty is also a factor. Having recently won her independence, Indonesia is determined not to lose freedom of action by tying herself to one bloc or the other.

Indonesia's foreign policy is based on taking an active role in trying to build peace in the world. To this end she sponsored the Asian-African Conference at Bandung this spring and has offered to mediate on the issue of Formosa Strait.

For a nation that has enjoyed but six years of independence and is beset with a multitude of domestic problems, this role in the eyes of some domestic critics is rather presumptuous.

The one national complaint that dominates much of the thinking in Indonesia's foreign policy is the matter of Netherlands New Guinea, or West Irian, as Indonesia calls that western territory of the great island of New Guinea.

That land on the east of the Republic of Indonesia is economically of little importance. But that it still remains in Dutch hands means for Indonesians—and particularly for the Indonesians in the present government—that a colonial power still clings to what they consider to be a part of their country.

But the central government, dominated as it is by the Javanese, does not have all Indonesia behind it on the issue of West Irian, or Netherlands New Guinea. For instance, the great island of the Celebes, east of Borneo, has many aspects of thought unlike the thought of Jakarta.

"What is the good of substituting for Dutch colonial rule in West Irian the Indonesian colonial rule?" a scholar in the Celebes says. "Do you honestly think there is anything to be gained by imposing the kind of irresponsible military rule we have here on the primitive people of West Irian?"

Despite the Indonesian Government's resentment of the United States for its neutral policy with regard to Netherlands

New Guinea, the feeling of the people in this country is basically friendly to the United States.

They are also aware of Communist China as a force in the Asian world that is close to them.

The effect of Communist Premier Chou En-lai's visit to this country during and just after the Bandung conference should not be underestimated. To the Indonesian Mr. Chou seemed a very reasonable statesman—a man with whom it would be quite possible to negotiate and work out agreements.

9. The Philippines

MAGSAYSAY: DYNAMIC EXAMPLE FOR ASIA [19]

How do you beat the Communists at their own game?

The world has been given a dramatic demonstration by President Ramón Magsaysay (pronounced Mahg-sigh-sigh) of the Philippines. Only a few years ago the Communist-dominated Huks were in control of the rich rice bowl of the Philippines, and their Moscow-trained leader, Luis Taruc, boasted an armed force of fifty thousand men backed by a reserve of two million. When Taruc gave arrogant notice that he would soon take over Manila and the government, Magsaysay was pressed into service as Minister of Defense. His mission was to revitalize that demoralized ministry, to purge the army of fifth columnists, to save the country.

Last May Taruc, defeated and discredited, surrendered unconditionally to Magsaysay. His followers, cut down to a few thousand surrounded fugitives in the swamps and hills, are no longer fed by credulous peasants or hidden by terrified villagers.

There is a profound lesson in this: when you cut the navel cord of support between the masses and a dissident group, the power of such a group to defy, subvert, or overthrow government withers away.

How did Magsaysay do this?

[19] From article by J. P. McEvoy, *Reader's Digest* roving editor. *Reader's Digest.* 65:107-11. September 1954. Reprinted by permission.

"When I was given the job of stopping the Huks," he told me, "I realized that I had this advantage: they were guerrillas and I, too, had been a guerrilla—against the Japanese. I knew you cannot beat guerrillas except by unorthodox tactics. So I launched an unorthodox campaign. Where they used terrorism, I used kindness—plus pesos. Anyone who brought me information I rewarded liberally. Also, I promised to give any Huk who deserted exactly what he claimed he was fighting for—land, house, rice.

"Then, when I ran for president last fall, I promised the people that I would do everything in my power to correct the age-old evils and injustices that made *new* Huks."

His opponents in the political campaign admitted that Magsaysay saved the country from the Communists. "But," they added, "he is a military man. If you elect him president he will know nothing about industry, trade, the compromises of domestic intrigue or the pitfalls of foreign relations."

But Magsaysay, campaigning with characteristic straightforward simplicity and tremendous energy, was elected by a record-breaking landslide. To get to the people, he rode trains and planes and buses and bull carts. He declared: "When I am president, if you have any grievance against any official or any department of the government, you can wire direct to me and you will get action."

True to his word, Magsaysay has set up a unique complaint department in Malacañang Palace. It sprawls over the ground floor of one wing, handles up to a thousand complaints per day. Anyone with a grievance can telegraph the president fifty words free of charge. Each complaint is acknowledged by a personal telegram from the president, and is recorded on a follow-up card index and routed to the proper official with a crisp admonition that amounts to "Snap out of that siesta, *amigo!*" . . .

Ramón Magsaysay is young (47), dark, dynamic. Big for a Filipino (a husky six-footer), he weaves like a boxer when he talks and is given to explosive gestures, lightning decisions and, as we have seen, unorthodox tactics. Add his personal charm, native shrewdness, unimpeachable honesty, a built-in radar that spots phonies at a glance, and you begin to understand his enormous popularity. . . .

What are Magsaysay's problems and what are his chances of succeeding? [Magsaysay says:]

Overpopulation is not one of our problems. . . . Whereas Japan has 579 persons to the square mile and Java has 1019, we have only 173. Our total population is around twenty million—for a country bigger than the British Isles. We have an abundance of rich soil and natural resources, a good climate, and experts tell me the land could support eighty million people if our problems, new and old, could be solved.

Unemployment is one of our biggest headaches. There is not enough irrigation, so only one rice crop per year is the general rule. Farmers, who are 75 per cent of the population, work less than half the year. Many could find employment if there were more local industries. But native capital is traditionally timid about new business ventures. Why risk unfamiliar hazards when you can doze the centuries away with the comparative security and low taxes of landed estates?

Which brings up our most paralyzing problems, defying solution so far: the landless man and the manless land.

Ninety per cent of our Philippine farmers are tenant share-croppers. They have no land of their own and usually nothing more than a verbal arrangement which can be terminated at any time. This feudal system is a legacy of three hundred years of Spanish rule. True, there are laws on the books designed to protect the tenants from exploitation, but they are easily evaded or defied: the tenant is helpless when faced with long and costly litigation. Unfair sharing, usury and other age-old abuses have lowered the morale of the farming masses until today the Filipino, whose basic food is rice, is just about the poorest individual rice-producer in the world.

Magsaysay's legislative program to correct these evils has had hard going. The most powerful legislators represent the biggest landowners; asking them to vote against themselves is what the Chinese call "negotiating with the tiger for his hide."

"As for manless land," says Magsaysay, "we have lots of it—publicly owned, fertile and idle. I am settling some of it with groups of repentant Huks and their wives and little Huklings." A typical community of the EDCOR (Economic Development Corps) project consists of hundreds of homes laid out in a kind of Far East Levittown, where everything needed is furnished by the government or by the army.

But Magsaysay knows that a giveaway program solves nothing permanently. He has asked Dr. James Yen, probably the world's most experienced authority on rural reconstruction, to advise him. [Yen told him:]

In some thirty years of experience in China, . . . I have learned that doing good for people, even with the best intentions, is not enough. They must be taught to help themselves. Otherwise you have *relief*, which is only temporary. What you want is *release*, which grows as the energies of the people themselves are stimulated and trained. The motive power in any mass movement must be the people themselves.

10. *Formosa*

CHIANG KAI-SHEK AND THE RETURN [20]

Chiang Kai-shek long ago found [that] the world's primary and implacable enemy was and is the Communist conspiracy directed from Moscow. It was a single-mindedness that in the 1930's exasperated his countrymen (who wanted him to fight Japanese instead of Communists), in the 1940's, General Joseph Stilwell (who wanted him to arm Communist troops to fight in Burma) and President Harry Truman (who insisted that he coalesce with what Secretary of State Byrnes termed "the so-called Communists"). . . No name among the world's leaders strikes such fierce sparks of antagonism or praise as the name of this austere, remote man on the cool veranda. To some he is a "discredited dictator" who lost China through his own short-comings; to others he is a "gallant ally" who was let down by the United States. . . .

In the United States, once itself deeply divided, the Congress recently approved all but unanimously a pledge of United States forces to the defense of Chiang's Formosa. Much of the rest of the world, if it had not changed its mind about Chiang, had changed its mind about the nature of the regime that overthrew him. Whatever some may think of Chiang personally . . . there is now wide agreement that Formosa should and must be saved

[20] From "Man of the Single Truth." *Time*. 65:32-9. April 18, 1955. Courtesy *Time* Magazine: copyright Time Inc. 1955.

as a bastion in the free world's defense. Said Australia's Prime Minister Robert Menzies in Washington a fortnight ago: "There are far too many people who have taken the easy course of thinking about these things in terms of some man or some name. We don't defend a man, we don't defend a system of government— we defend a nation against tyranny from abroad." . . .

[In April 1955] Communist artillerymen on the mainland dropped shells onto the rice fields of Quemoy, splashed other shells among the Matsus' fishing boats. Facing the Communists were three well-trained and well-dug-in Nationalist divisions on Big and Little Quemoy, another division in the Matsus, 150 miles to the north. While the United States wrestled with itself over the problem of intervening, and the United States' allies wrung their hands in dismay at the prospect, Chiang insisted calmly that the offshore islands would be defended by him to the last man— whatever his ally might do. [Says Chiang:]

Our army must not be asked to abandon another front, or voluntarily participate in another retreat. To abandon another front without a fight would betray [my soldiers'] confidence and endanger their loyalty. Our government could sustain a defeat on a single front, and maintain its morale and will to fight. But we might not do so if we retreat without a fight. We can and will fight on, even without assistance of allies, so long as morale remains high. Should our morale be destroyed, even our friends would be unable to help us. . . .

Chiang is highly conscious that his governance of Formosa can establish his best claim to, and justification for, a return to the mainland—or blight that hope forever. In his twenty-two years as head of the Nationalist government on the mainland, Chiang never had a year when he was not fighting either war lords, Communists, or the Japanese. In the last four years on Formosa, he has had a chance to show what the Nationalists might have done if they had had peace. . . .

The Formosans had no cause to love the two million defeated Nationalists who descended on them at the bitter end of 1949. The first Nationalist governor to take over from the Japanese at war's end had arrived with a retinue of carpetbaggers and incompetents. In 1947 a rebellion flared which lasted three days, was bloodily put down by General Peng Meng-chi, then commander of the Nationalist garrison and now acting chief of the general staff. Thousands were killed.

Chiang moved swiftly to restore Formosan morale. He installed as governor frail, ulcer-ridden Chen Cheng, a general turned civilian who had been with Chiang since student days. Chen simultaneously tightened police control and initiated basic reforms, notably land reform. Chiang had learned his lesson on the mainland: "The consensus is that our party failed during the past four years because we failed to enforce the principle of the people's livelihood."

Laws were passed limiting rents, which had ranged as high as 70 per cent of the year's crop, to 37.5 per cent. The government broke up and sold off the big landholdings inherited from the Japanese; it bought land from the landlords and resold it to tenants on easy terms. In four years of Chiang's rule, tenancy has been reduced from 40 per cent to 20 per cent, and thousands of Formosans built "37.5 per cent houses" and took "37.5 per cent brides."

Chiang's new land is no mean property. With the two million Nationalists added to its native population of eight million (most of them descended from Chinese refugees from the Manchus in the seventeenth century), Formosa is about as big in area and population as either Belgium or the Netherlands. Before the war, its standard of living was second only to Japan's in the Orient; it was the world's second largest exporter of sugar, and its total exports (rice, tea, fruit) exceeded Turkey's or Yugoslavia's. With big help from United States experts and greenbacks, Formosa's economy has thrived. Electric power has been doubled, production of fertilizer increased sixfold, textiles twelvefold. The Formosan dollar has proved more stable than the Japanese yen, has been nearly stable since 1950. Nine out of ten Formosan children are now in schools (versus 71 per cent under Japanese), and public schools were established in the mountainous regions where Formosa's 150,000 aborigines dwell.

Politically, Formosans are getting a bigger and bigger hand in their own government: four years ago, elections were instituted for local posts. Last year the provincial assembly itself was elected by popular vote. In many elections, "independents" opposed the Kuomintang's candidates, and recently in some important instances, *e.g.*, mayor of Taipei, the independents have won.

There are still difficulties. The Nationalists crowd the island, they have an air of superiority, they find it hard to understand the Fukienese dialect the Formosans speak, and Formosans dislike having to learn Mandarin just a few years after having to learn Japanese. . . . But intermarriages are on the increase. Most significantly, beginning last year native Formosan boys were drafted into the army to replace the Nationalists' aging veterans. There was no trouble, and the Nationalist army now has ninety thousand such troops. . . .

Chiang Kai-shek still runs a one-party national government, and in many respects a one-man government. He is President of China, director-general of the Kuomintang, and commander in chief of the armed forces. But primarily, his power rests on the reverence, respect and fear which he inspires and commands in his own person.

Chiang cannot always have his way. Often he must cajole and buy his way. Sometimes he must submit to pressures, as he did in 1950 when the younger Nationalist generation forced him to retire hundreds of old Kuomintang wheelhorses to sinecures. Chiang accepted and compelled the evacuation of the Tachen Islands only over the violent protests of many of his ministers.

The national government has been progressively diminished as the provincial government of Formosa has increased its independence, until today there are only 12,000 employees in the national government versus 113,000 in the provincial government. Except for Foreign Affairs and the Defense Ministry, most of the national ministries, their functions duplicated by provincial departments, are only skeleton organizations with nothing to do but plan for the day of the return. . . .

Closest of all Chiang's advisers is still Wellesley-educated Madame Chiang. She is not as influential as she once was, and her patronage is no longer regarded as the sure road to preference. She repairs every day to her office of her "Chinese Women's Anti-Aggression League," to which she can and does summon ministers at will. "My role is very simple," she explains. "I assist my husband."

And there is his son, Chiang Ching-kuo, by an earlier marriage. The son's formal title is Deputy Secretary-General of the National Defense Council, but his real duties are as his father's troubleshooter. As head of the secret police and boss of the political officers in the armed forces, the son is chief guardian of the island's political security. As such, he is the most widely feared man on the island. A burly man of 46, Ching-kuo explains: "You must always remember that we have an enemy."

The danger is real: the Communists have tried hard to subvert Formosan loyalty. Three years ago a vice chief of staff was discovered to be a Communist spy. A few months ago two student pilots flew off to the Chinese mainland with an airforce trainer. But Chiang Ching-kuo insists that security cases are now down to two or three a month.

Formosa is not as politically free as the Philippines or Japan, but it is freer than South Korea. The press can and does criticize, so long as it does not appear to Chiang Kai-shek as obstructing the national effort or damaging the prestige of the government. After all, Chiang reminds critics, "we are at war." . . .

On Formosa, some have lost all faith in the return. They recognize that they are not going back to the mainland unless the United States helps put them there. They argue that the government should concentrate on making Formosa a viable place, that the hope of return, constantly frustrated, leads to nothing but despair.

But the President of Nationalist China will hear no talk of settling down on a neutralized Formosa. Chiang Kai-shek does not believe this is one of the possibilities open to him or to the world, no matter how much well-intentioned diplomats try to bring off a settlement. On this basic point he and his Communist enemy (to judge by the enemy's words) are in complete agreement.

Does this mean that Chiang accepts—and would even wish to bring on—World War III? Today's world might not be prepared to accept Chiang's answer, for it runs counter to accepted habits of thought. His "counterattack" on the mainland, says Chiang Kai-shek, will not bring on a general war: in fact,

it is the only way World War III can be avoided, for so long
as the mainland of China is in Communist hands, a third world
war will always be possible and perhaps likely.

STRATEGY OF FORMOSA [21]

When President Eisenhower asked Congress for authority to
act in emergency to protect Formosa and the Pescadores, one of
the reasons he advanced was that "it was important that these
islands should remain in friendly hands." His use of the word
"important," rather than "essential" or "vital," had more significance than is generally realized.

Military planners distinguish very carefully among these
terms in their appreciations. "Important" means to them what
it means to anyone. A position can be important, yet not essential or vital. "Essential" is used militarily with regard usually
to a specific operation, area, or circumstance. "Vital" is the
highest category and is used only of a position whose loss would
be a mortal threat. There are very few areas in the world that
our planners consider vital.

When the President used "important" to indicate the strategic value of Formosa to the United States and to the other
Far Eastern countries friendly to us, he took a moderate position.
"In unfriendly hands," he declared, ". . . It would create a
breach in the island chain of the western Pacific that constitutes,
for the United States and other free nations, the geographical
backbone of their security structure in that ocean. In addition,
this breach would interrupt north-south communications between
other important elements of that barrier . . ."

The barrier the President spoke of is the island chain extending about three thousand miles from north to south off the coast
of Asia, including the Japanese home islands, the Ryukyus, Formosa, and the Philippines. Formosa is slightly south of the
center of this chain of islands and is closest of all to the main-

[21] From "An Important Link in the Chain," article by Thomas R. Phillips,
brigadier general, United States Army (retired). *Reporter*. 12:19-20. March
10, 1955. Reprinted by permission.

land—even closer than Japan is to the Korean peninsula. . . .

Under the new concept of defense in the western Pacific, the barrier chain will become the advanced line of radar-warning and interceptor bases to protect our striking power based farther east. Radar and interceptors will be manned by Japanese, Chiang's Chinese, and Filipinos.

Viewed in this light, Formosa plays an important part in the defensive chain, now complete without any large breaks. If Formosa were seized by the Reds, there would be a gap of about 660 miles between the Philippines and Okinawa. This is too large to be bridged by radar and interceptors. Although the Ryukyus extend another 275 miles south from Okinawa and the Bataan islands extend north 165 miles from the Philippines, leaving a gap of only about 275 miles, these small islands would not be tenable against powerful air forces on Formosa.

Formosa is now a flank position that threatens any Communist move toward the Philippines to the south or Japan and Okinawa to the north. If the Reds were to move into Southeast Asia by land, the troops on Formosa would constitute a threat of invasion that the Communists would have to be prepared to cope with by leaving large forces opposite the island.

Let us examine the reasons given by certain authorities to prove the strategic importance of Formosa. At present any talk of a Red invasion of the Philippines or Okinawa and Japan is unrealistic. The Communists do not have the naval vessels to cover an operation so distant from the mainland or the air force to protect it at that range. Nor is there any cause for worry about the air-warning and air-defense barriers to protect Guam, for the Chinese Reds have no aircraft now that can reach out so far.

But this reason, which is presently being adduced by the military advisers to the Secretary of State, will be quite valid when the Red Chinese have a more highly developed military establishment. Their final reason—that possession of Formosa by our ally Chiang is a threat to the mainland that would have to be taken care of if the Reds were at war in Indo-China or Korea—is valid today and will remain valid as long as we retain superior air and sea power in the western Pacific. To the

Reds, Formosa is a mortal threat, just as uninvaded Britain was a mortal threat to Hitler.

Hitler put off his problem and it sealed his fate. The Chinese Reds may be forced to put off the solution of their troubles by lack of military power, the restraint of their Soviet ally, or possibly by international action to neutralize Formosa.

Although the President found Formosa "important" to the United States strategically in the area of the western Pacific, the National Security Council, on the basis of other considerations and following military advice, found it "essential" to our overall strategy for stopping Communist expansion. It was felt that we could not lose any threatened territory to communism and retain the confidence of other nations, such as south Vietnam, Cambodia, Thailand, and Burma, that are subject to Communist pressure.

The degree of essentiality in military semantics also came up in connection with the problem of whether to defend the offshore islands—the Tachens, Matsu, and Quemoy. All four of the Joint Chiefs of Staff testified separately before the Senate Foreign Relations and Armed Services Committees that Quemoy and Matsu were not vital to the defense of Formosa. Important, yes—and the different Chiefs ascribed varying degrees of importance to them—but not "vital" or "essential."

It will be years—five or ten—before the Red Chinese can build up their naval and air forces to a degree that will give them a chance of making a successful invasion of Formosa. They can make a stab at invading the off-shore islands this year. Therefore the two problems—invasion of the offshore islands and invasion of Formosa—are, in the jargon of science fiction, on different time lines. Taking the offshore islands this year would have no connection with invading Formosa five years from now. The Red propaganda attempt to relate the two is phony. . . .

If the question of Formosa is projected five to ten years ahead, when we can assume that the Chinese Communists will have acquired a short-range navy and a larger air force with medium bombers and atomic weapons, a different strategic picture appears. Formosa can receive only six minutes' radar warning of the approach of jets across the Strait. This would make its defense against bombing attack almost impossible, for defensive interceptors could not take off and gain altitude in that time. . . .

In short, Formosa will have no strategic value to us if Red Chinese military development continues at its present rate. On the other hand, if the Reds held the island, our bombing forces from the fleet and the Pacific islands could neutralize it.

Thus we can see how different the defense of Formosa was when former President Truman ordered the Seventh Fleet to protect it in June 1950. That was a simple military problem; a destroyer and a few patrol craft were all that was required. As the Red navy and air force increase, however, the once easy job will become a major military burden. Our fleet in the western Pacific will have to be enlarged. More air bases will have to be constructed and more aircraft made available. More ground forces will be needed to defend bases.

Barring unforeseen change in the western Pacific, or the neutralization of Formosa by international agreement, it seems to me that ultimately the Reds must attempt to take it. Ideology and nationalism apart, for them it is strategically "vital."

Today the defense of Formosa is strategically "important" to us and "essential" in our anti-Communist global strategy. But as time goes by and Red Chinese military power grows, the defense will become increasingly risky and impossibly burdensome unless we recognize the problem and seek a solution not prompted by our own outraged feelings.

The once simple problem of protecting Formosa is, I fear, evolving into an insoluble conflict that almost irrevocably will lead us into war.

11. *Korea*

THE UNITED STATES STAKE IN DIVIDED KOREA [22]

For its size South Korea is America's most expensive stepchild. The $700 million we are contributing this fiscal year

[22] From "Foreign Affairs: South Korea's Future Is Obscure," column by C. L. Sulzberger, New York *Times* chief foreign correspondent. New York *Times*. p28. April 4, 1955. Reprinted by permission.

[1954-1955] represents about half the Republic's gross national product. In exchange our security is reinforced by a courageous army of twenty regular and ten reserve divisions.

One immediate goal is to keep Syngman Rhee sufficiently strong to repel invasion but sufficiently shackled to prevent him from seizing the initiative and starting another war. We ration his fuel and ammunition and reserve to ourselves the major air-support role.

If the cold war lasts much longer we may find it uneconomic to continue financing a massive South Korean Army. Already, bound by armistice restrictions, we have had to gum up our own production lines to keep manufacturing spare parts for President Rhee's outmoded tanks which cannot be replaced by new models. Meanwhile, there are many indications the Communists in the North violate truce terms. United Nations observers report each week the departure for Manchuria of hundreds of empty box cars never checked into the country. Cynics remark that North Korea must surely be the world's largest manufacturer of rolling stock. Lieutenant General Kim Chung Yul, Syngman Rhee's air force commander, says the Communists have built up a jet strength of 255 MIG-15 fighters and eighty-four IL-28 medium bombers.

To offset this we must not only maintain the South Korean Army but support it with our mobile strength from Japanese island bases. Over any protracted period this will be impracticable as President Rhee himself takes pains to stress in somewhat hysterical terms. The United States is already encouraging Japan to build up its defense forces so that, within perhaps five years, we can pull back from the bases we maintain there. The Japanese will start manufacturing Sabre jets this summer.

Japan has considerable industry and already manufactures military transport, weapons and ammunition. Where, Dr. Rhee wonders, will this eventually leave Korea? He envisions the day when he will have to depend on his ancient enemy for air, sea and logistical support. And he refuses to accept such a position. Yet South Korea cannot do much more militarily than provide manpower. It has no industry worth mentioning nor the necessary skilled workers. It can never build automobiles or aircraft within a foreseeable period. Therefore, if our plans eventually materialize into withdrawal from Japan, South Korea will feel naked.

This country is rich in energy, determination and patriotism, but poor in other things. Japan occupied it forty years and deliberately destroyed its intelligentsia, restricted educational facilities and left no bureaucratic personnel. . . . In Pusan the Minister of Foreign Affairs, Minister of Defense and Chief of Staff told me that before the war their respective jobs had been high school teacher, sailor in Japan's merchant fleet and captain in Japanese cavalry.

South Korea has had only two years of truly independent government—between the end of American military administration in 1948 and the start of war in 1950. Yet progress has been made despite over-zealous police, a warped economy and the wreckage of destructive battles. There is considerable press freedom notwithstanding President Rhee's fitful personal censorship. Debates in Parliament are vigorous.

But the economy is an impossible mess. We hope gradually to reduce our contribution to about $250 million per annum, but the date when that can be done safely seems far off. Inflation is rampant and usury rife. Monthly interest rates run as high as 20 per cent. By political blackmail and a rather engaging personality Syngman Rhee has managed to win unreasonable favors from us. He insists we finance his defense force totally. Yet South Korea finds enough spare money to dabble in television and Cinemascope projects. The President violates agreements with us when it suits him.

President Rhee is unabashedly anxious to start a new hot war. He sees the way signs are pointing: Gradual diminution of American strength in favor of Japanese build-up, a hopeless economy, the fact that he himself, now 80, has not long to live. And without Dr. Rhee, embarrassing as he can be at times, it is hard to imagine a South Korean government. In any election minus his ebullient personality the fellow-traveling Left might win. The Right majority would be hopelessly split.

This country cannot exist indefinitely, above all on a partitioned basis, unless the United States maintains its present rate

of financial aid—which is unlikely. Yet we have pledged ourselves to rehabilitate South Korea, come what may. Our investment in blood, money and promises is immense. It is hard to
conjecture how we can make it pay off.

BARRIER AGAINST COMMUNISM [23]

Five years ago the North Korean army attacked across the
thirty-eighth parallel and overwhelmed the internal security force
the United States had helped the Republic of Korea raise and
train. Today any attempt to invade this strategic peninsula
should tell a different story.

Korean manpower and United States dollars have raised here
a barrier that looks like the strongest the free world has anywhere it faces communism across a common frontier. Since
the armistice of July 27, 1953, silenced the guns across Korea,
the United States has contributed $720 million in military aid to
this youngest of new republics. For its part, the Republic of
Korea has raised an army of 661,000, well-trained, well-armed,
with the will to fight—a small air force that soon will be armed
with jet fighters, and a navy of 13,000 men and forty ships that
is taking over from United Nations' naval forces the task of
patroling Korea's long coastline.

Many Americans still may remember the ease with which the
Soviet-trained and equipped North Korean forces swept almost
to Pusan in the summer of 1950. Or other days when under-
armed, undertrained Korean troops broke under the Communist
attacks that always were aimed at their positions if they held a
common front.

You can forget the past, say American officers who have
lived and worked with the Koreans for the last two years and
who should know them best.

"What did we expect during the war?" they ask. "A
miracle?"

[23] From "Five Years Harden Troops of Korea," news story by Foster Hailey,
New York *Times* staff correspondent. New York *Times*. p4. June 10, 1955. Reprinted by permission.

This is an army and a navy and an air force that know how to fight, has the will to do so and that would be more than a match for any like Asian force that could be sent against it, the American officers say.

The 661,000-man ground force is the largest on the free world side after that of the United States.

Skepticism fades before the visual evidence that confronts a visitor on a five-day tour of Korean military installations.

From drill teams at headquarters in Seoul or at First Army headquarters in Wonju, through front-line bunkers, replacement training centers, army, navy and air force academies, the general staff college and supply installations, the Republic of Korea forces look, act and talk like an outfit that knows its business.

Most impressive of all is the affectionate admiration with which every United States military adviser who has been here longer than two weeks speaks of "my ROK's."

"The finest army in the world," says Major General R. L. Howze, who headed the United States Army advisory group from last September until he was relieved last week to return to the States.

Major General Harlan C. Parks of the United States Air Force, says the Korean air arm headed by Lieutenant General Ung Yul is "a slick little air force."

"These are keen boys," says Ensign Charles Manellis of the United States Navy as he takes a visitor through the Korean naval academy at Chinhae, which has a capacity of two hundred new midshipmen each year.

"They do things like we do," says Captain Joseph F. Holzbauer of the United States Marine Corps as he explains the Korean marine corps schools.

The Navy academy wanted a seaplane and did not have the money to buy one. So it built one—from plans clipped from an American magazine, *Popular Mechanics*.

"And the damn thing flies," said an incredulous American officer.

Nine weeks after a boy from the paddies marches through the gates at the Nonsan Training Center he is crawling along the ground under machine-gun fire with two-pound powder charges exploding all around him. And showing no panic.

Four-star generals who were too busy fighting to stop and learn the ABC's of their business can be found in schools poring over signal apparatus or automotive maintenance books, seeking knowledge most American boys learned in the Boy Scouts and from operating their own hot rods in high school days.

In addition to raising a military barrier against aggression, the Korean military forces also are a very real factor in raising educational levels, in dragging Korea from the stagnation of hundreds of years in the frightening new atomic world.

In a bunker fifty feet back from an aperture looking two and one-half miles across the demilitarized zone to the Communist line, a class of thirty men was seen learning to read and write their own language. After this comes compulsory English courses.

12. *Japan*

ALLY WITH PROBLEMS [24]

There is great difference of opinion within Japan as to what policy should be pursued with respect to rearmament. Many believe Japan cannot afford an armed establishment of sufficient size to provide it with security and that the safest policy is not to rearm. For a variety of reasons popular sentiment is opposed to rearmament. Nevertheless, the United States has continued to press the Japanese Government for an increase in the size of the security force. This is . . . so volatile an issue that it might easily cause the overthrow of Japanese governments. . . .

Since the end of the occupation there has been a marked growth of nationalist groups in Japan. Some of the old prewar patriotic groups have been revived, and new groups have been formed. The trend has not as yet reached important proportions, but a nationalist reaction is bound to come in Japan. It may be

[24] From *The New Japan*, pamphlet by Royden Dangerfield, professor of political science and director of the Institute of Government and Public Affairs at the University of Illinois. (Headline Series no 102) Foreign Policy Association. New York. November-December 1953. p50-5. Reprinted by permission.

a new nationalism based on Japan's culture; or nationalism may be captured by the militarist-minded and the chauvinist. The revival of reaction may become a troublesome problem for the Japanese.

Much fear has been expressed about the rise of communism in Japan. In the 1949 election Communist candidates polled nearly 10 per cent of the vote; Communists were important in the labor unions; and the Communist party showed a striking increase in membership. But the Communist threat appears to have subsided. . . .

The attitude of the Japanese toward the United States is affected by the fact that the two countries are closely allied. Under rights granted in the security treaty, the United States maintains military, naval and air bases in Japan. Many Japanese feel that the existence of such bases on its territory constitutes a menace to Japan. They reason that the Soviet Union must view such installations as a threat and therefore must consider Japan an enemy. The left-wing parties have utilized this argument effectively. Many leaders of Japanese thought are neutralists and believe that the security and well-being of Japan are best promoted if their country is not committed to either side. The security treaty is thus an issue in both domestic and foreign affairs. . . .

Japan has not yet solved the problem of political relations with many peoples against whom it fought in the Pacific war. The Indonesians, the Vietnamese, the Filipinos and the Koreans are both fearful and distrustful of the Japanese. This has been manifest in many ways. The peace treaty signed with Japan was unsatisfactory to the countries of Southeast Asia. Japanese businessmen have found it extremely difficult to do business in the area. Nor has the Japanese Government found it easy to establish amicable relations with Dr. Syngman Rhee's government in South Korea. The scars of the war persist. The question of reparations for war damage caused to Asian countries by Japanese conquest will continue to be a major problem for some time.

The future of Japan will be determined in large part by the nature of its relations with the mainland of Asia. Since Japan is allied with and under the influence of the United States and since this country is engaged in conflict, both hot and cold, with Communist China, the relations between Japan and China are not at present on a basis which could promote the future interests of Japan. Tokyo's problem is how to develop trade and better political relations with Communist China and at the same time continue its very necessary relations with the United States. This is a dilemma which the Japanese recognize but for which no solution has as yet been found.

Being allied with the United States, Japan is engaged in the cold war against the Soviet Union. Since the Kremlin controls Sakhalin and the Kuriles, both within a very short distance from the Japanese islands, it is extremely important to Japan that relations with the USSR be peaceful, if not cordial. . . .

The economic future of Japan unquestionably depends to a major degree on the development of trade with the China mainland. If the Peiping regime remains in control, Japan will have to decide whether or not to establish relations with Communist China. This could be done if Japan were free from the restricting influence of the United States. But Japan is committed to the West. In this ambivalent situation it experiences frustration and indecision.

Will Japan continue to collaborate with the United States and the free world? The United States has endeavored to rebuild Japan as the bulwark against communism in the Far East. Under the conditions of the cold war and the facts of practical politics, Japan has become an ally of the West. It will continue to play that role if the condition of its economy permits; and the future economic position of Japan will depend in large part on policies pursued by the nations of the free world. Should its economic condition deteriorate to a serious extent, Japan might find it necessary to look elsewhere for the trade opportunities which the relations with the free world have so far failed to produce.

The Soviet Union has hitherto pursued a policy toward Japan which has precluded any rapprochement. Should Moscow so desire, it is in a position to give the Japanese an opportunity for more favorable trade and political relations with the Soviet Union and with Communist China. In the future the Kremlin may undertake to promote such relations. Should this happen, the Japanese would face a crucial and fateful choice between the Communist and non-Communist orbits. Again, the answer will be profoundly influenced by the condition of the Japanese economy at the time the choice becomes imperative.

The United States should exert every effort to make certain that the nations of the free world grant to the Japanese the freest possible access to raw materials and markets so essential to their economic well-being. Given such access, the Japanese possess the ability to solve their own difficulties. The solution of the economic problem would produce a more stable internal political situation and would permanently link Japan to the free world.

JAPAN'S POLITICS [25]

Ichiro Hatoyama is a smooth and resilient seventy-two-year-old veteran of Japanese politics. A rich man closely connected with industrial and banking circles, he is bitterly anti-Communist. But because he was briefly purged from political life as a pro-Fascist by the United States Occupation, he is considered by many Japanese a symbol of resistance to United States domination. When the strongly pro-American government of Premier Yoshida fell last December, Mr. Hatoyama became premier of a caretaker government. In general elections [February 27, 1955], Japanese voters made it a . . . certainty Mr. Hatoyama would be named premier again. . . .

The campaign turned on two main foreign policy issues— full-fledged rearmament as a contribution to free world strength, and relations with the Communist world.

Four major parties figured in maneuvers around these issues. Two on the left—the Left Socialists and Right Socialists—came out against rearmament and for closer ties with the Communists. Former Premier Yoshida's Liberal party, on the right, favored rearmament and was cautious on relations with the Communists. Mr. Hatoyama placed his Democratic party

[25] From "Victory for Hatoyama," news story. New York *Times*. p E2. Mr. 6, '55. Reprinted by permission.

squarely behind closer ties to Moscow and rearmament. . . .
[The Liberals and Democrats won 297 of the seats in Japan's
467-member lower house.]

After the votes were tabulated, the Liberals announced they
would team up with the Democrats to assure Mr. Hatoyama a
stable majority. Mr. Hatoyama said that "efforts to adjust relations with Russia will be continued." But the Hatoyama majority falls short of the two-thirds margin necessary to push through
full-fledged rearmament which must be treated as a constitutional
amendment. "No revision in the constitution," Mr. Hatoyama
said, "can be accomplished for some time."

The apparent upshot of the elections is that Japan is moving
toward a more "independent" cold war position—limiting her
armament, and "adjusting" to the existence of Communist
power. But Mr. Hatoyama's known anti-communism makes it
plain that whatever the adjustment, Japan, basically, will remain
aligned with the free world against the Communists.

JAPAN'S ECONOMIC TEST [26]

It is perhaps no exaggeration to contend that the course
which Japanese-American relations will take in the future will
depend largely on the course which the Japanese economy will
take. That is to say, if Japan's "free" economy can continue to
prosper reasonably and meet the basic living requirements of
the Japanese people, then Japanese-American relations should
remain on a cordial basis and possibly become even more cordial.
However, if Japan's "free" economy cannot meet the basic living requirements of the Japanese people, then one can almost
be certain that the extremists will gain control of the government
and that relations between the United States and Japan will
deteriorate rapidly and probably in the end be characterized by
open friction and hostility. . . .

[26] From *Japan and America*, by Lawrence H. Battistini, author, historian, and
former economist for the civil historical section of SCAP, General MacArthur's occupation staff. John Day Co. New York. 1954. p 171-6. Copyright 1953 by
Lawrence H. Battistini. Reprinted by permission.

The new Japan . . . has shown more than a mere token willingness to cooperate with the United States within the framework of basic American world and Far Eastern policy, often to the partial detriment of Japan. For example, the [Japanese] government has shunned the strong temptation to "do business" with Red China on a large scale despite the fact that China and Japan are at present natural trading countries and will probably remain so for another generation or two, if not longer. This self-denial was obviously accepted by the . . . government for two main reasons: (1) a genuine fear and distrust of communism and Communist state power as represented by Soviet Russia and Red China; and (2) a feeling, and strong hope, that temporary sacrifices by Japan would be fully, or nearly fully, compensated for by economic assistance from the United States and American help for the Japanese economy in the form of enlightened trade policies.

Any attempt to predict the course of future events, of course, is risky and moreover pointless, as there are too many variables and intangibles involved which have a bearing on the future of Japanese-American relations. However, one prediction can safely be made. If Japan does not have free and equal access to sources of raw materials and markets, the Japanese economy will collapse and the country may become confronted with the most serious economic crisis in its history. One should never lose sight of the fact that Japan has a vast population of some eighty-seven millions densely crowded on mountainous islands of less than 150,000 square miles, poor in minerals and with an arable area of less than 16 per cent of the total. This huge population is twenty-three millions more than it was in 1930, and is currently increasing at the rate of well over a million each year. If peace comes to the world and a world-wide depression takes place, and if with it the United States and other "have" nations again resort to ruthlessly high tariffs and crushing trade restrictions, then one can almost be certain that pro-American orientation will collapse like a house of cards. One can be equally certain in such a case that either the extreme Left or the extreme Right will successfully exploit the widespread misery and discontent and seize power with their promises of better days ahead if the nation will definitively turn its back on the policy of cooperation with the United States and wholeheartedly support their radical and chauvinistic policies.

No people, least of all the Japanese, will remain supine while their industries come to a halt, their wharves become silent, and the shadow of economic distress, suffering and hunger creeps over the land. . . . Japan's economic future is dark, very dark, and almost but not quite hopeless. This is an unpleasant fact that must be squarely faced, particularly by Americans and their government. The United States cannot, of course, be expected to assume responsibility for the huge and teeming Japanese population, or for the smallness of the Japanese islands and their paucity of resources. Neither can the United States be expected to compensate Japan for the loss of its once rich and far-flung empire. The United States obviously could not be expected to assume these responsibilities or make these compensations because it simply does not have the means to do so. However, the United States can, and must, make certain small and perhaps temporary sacrifices and adopt trade and general cosmopolitan policies which among other things will continually encourage the flow of imports and exports among all free countries. Only by such sacrifices and policies can the United States do its urgently required part to give the Japanese "free" economy a fighting chance for survival. . . .

Japan did not suddenly spring to life with the arrival of General MacArthur in September 1945. Japan has had a long history, much longer than that of the United States, and longer even than that of any present Western European state. Through their hard work, sacrifices, and particular abilities the Japanese succeeded in fashioning the strongest state in Asia. For nearly half a century Japan stood forth as the equal of any Western power. By following their militarists and ultranationalists the Japanese succeeded in building a rich and powerful empire, with which they enjoyed by far the highest standard of living in Asia and the promise of it continuing to increase. That empire and that standard of living were obtained by denouncing solemn treaties and resorting to wars and aggression. When and if the truly dark and difficult days descend on Japan, that empire will serve as a tempting reminder of the material riches that can be obtained if a nation will but make the temporary sacrifices and support a warlike government which does not hesitate to employ arms against its neighbors. The new world order which all of us of truly democratic leanings hope for and work for must demonstrate to the Japanese people, by deeds, that there is another way to survive, live, and prosper. And the United States, the most richly endowed of all the free countries and its leader by choice as well as destiny, must take the initiative in effectively demonstrating to the Japanese that it is to their advantage to be and remain a part of a free, unified, peaceful, one-world trading area.

The Japanese people are not by nature a defeatist people. Although crushed in the great Pacific war and humbled by a long occupation, Japan has arisen from the ashes of total defeat and again stands forth as the busiest and most highly industrialized nation of Asia. The third Tokyo, that amazing metropolis of steel and concrete which has arisen from the ashes and rubble of World War II, is symbolic of the dream of new Japan: belief in a future with work for all and reasonable security from want and fear. By nature the Japanese instinctively believe in and work for a future. Either the United States will help them find this future of a decent standard of living and reasonable economic cooperation with the United States, or Japan will ultimately take her own road. That road might conceivably lead to communism and integration of the Japanese economy in a Communist-world, planned-trading area, or it might lead the Japanese people to a detour where the trumpet calls of the ultra-nationalists and militarists might lure them on a long hike over a trail like the one which led to Pearl Harbor.

III. OUR ECONOMIC PROGRAM

EDITOR'S INTRODUCTION

Philosopher Bertrand Russell once wrote that there are three kinds of power—military, economic, and ideological (or political)—and that under the right circumstances each kind can be converted into one of the others. These changes, he said, are something like the transformation of one form of energy into another in physics. And the study of power, Russell added, was the essence of political science.

Russell's three forms of power and their transformation one into another occur over and over again in current world politics. Asian Communists, with their Marxist system of ideas, have been able to capture the minds of Indo-Chinese villagers, recruiting guerrilla fighting forces by citing existing grievances and offering glittering promises of reform. After this conversion of ideological power into military strength, the Communists go on to capture economic resources—the rich rice deltas of north Vietnam, for instance.

The United States, on the other hand, has used its economic power in assistance programs that have helped to save Western Europe from communism and that are now being used in Asia for the same purpose. The West, with its heritage of freedom and democracy, has had its successes on the ideological front also; Western nations are far from defenseless in combatting the appeals of communism. The trouble is that these appeals, false though they may be, often have a strong attraction for the peoples of underdeveloped lands emerging from colonial rule.

A considerable part of the debate about United States policy in Asia has to do with the degrees of emphasis we ought to put on military, economic, and ideological methods. Few voices are raised asking for the end of all economic assistance to Asia; still fewer want us to abandon the various ways of increasing our military strength in the Far East; nor do most critics of our foreign policy suggest that we ought to give up the information programs, diplomacy, and other means of persuasion by which we attempt to win friends for the United States and its ideals. But there are many, many differences about how much emphasis each of these approaches should receive.

And we still have much to learn about how one form of power is converted into another: "Politics," said Albert Einstein, "is more difficult to understand than physics." Therefore, there are many different opinions about how to carry out each approach. Some critics contend that we are spending too much time, money and attention on military methods. Others say that the economic approach is often futile because it will not win over countries like India. Others argue that Asians will rally to our cause only if we demonstrate military strength and firmness.

This section of this book presents various points of view on our economic program. Section IV, which follows, presents the arguments in regard to the military and ideological factors in our policy-making. The discussion of our economic program is given more space and includes more views than the other two subjects for several reasons. First, the whole idea of using economic assistance on a massive scale as an instrument of foreign policy is relatively new, inaugurated with the Marshall Plan in 1947. Then too, our aid program is probably the biggest variable in our foreign-policy equation: we can decide for ourselves how much aid we can give in what form to whom. Also, it is natural and inevitable that we ask ourselves at frequent intervals how much foreign aid we can afford, whether we should replace grants with loans, whether we can expect private investment to take over a greater portion of the task, and so forth.

Another reason is that our aid program has just undergone a substantial transformation. In 1953 Congress abolished the Mutual Security Agency (itself a successor to the Economic Cooperation Administration which administered the Marshall Plan) and replaced it with the Foreign Operations Administration. The FOA also took over the technical assistance program being carried out by the State Department—the "Point Four" program for underdeveloped countries initiated by President Truman in his 1949 inaugural message. In its 1954 foreign aid legislation,

Congress included a provision calling for termination of the FOA by June 30, 1955. Even though the agency was thus scheduled to go out of business, President Eisenhower recommended to Congress in April 1955 an expanded assistance program, with renewed emphasis on Asia, for the 1955-1956 fiscal year. Congress complied with this request, and most of the FOA's functions were taken over by a new International Cooperation Administration, set up as a semi-autonomous unit in the State Department. The President's request for $3.27 billion in new funds for the 1956 program was cut to $2.7 billion, but the use of funds already appropriated in previous years but not yet spent was expected to fill the gap. One of the largest items in the total appropriation was $800 million for "defense support" assistance to Asian countries—aid designed to put economic sinews behind the military efforts of free Asian countries.

The following articles present the reasons given by Administration spokesmen for the current economic assistance program, the views of two critics strongly opposed to the program, and other opinions favoring less drastic changes in emphasis or procedures.

OUR ECONOMIC STAKE IN ASIA [1]

In Asia the Communists have sharply stepped up subversive activities and with increasing intensity have preyed upon the honest aspirations of the people and attempted to perpetuate and magnify the remnants of antagonism engendered by years of colonialism. In most cases the young governments are not yet firmly established, political institutions are not fully matured and there is a severe shortage of trained public servants. By exploiting misery and perverting hopes, the Communists have tempted decent men, trying desperately to pull additional millions into the Soviet-slave orbit.

[1] From address by Harold E. Stassen, former director of the Foreign Operations Administration and now Special Assistant to the President on Disarmament, delivered before an AMVETS banquet, Washington, D.C., December 10, 1954. Mimeographed text supplied by Foreign Operations Administration. Reprinted by permission.

Wherever we have carried on joint programs with independent nations—programs of technical cooperation to share knowledge, of economic assistance to buttress economies, and of military support to strengthen defense, we have seen convincing evidence that these lesser developed nations and their peoples can become capable of standing on their own feet—that they can, as free men, greet the dawn of a new opportunity.

This was vividly demonstrated in the Manila Conference last September when both Western and Asian participants swiftly agreed upon a new Pacific Charter [Southeast Asia Treaty Organization] to serve as a foundation for the development of defensive strength and economic progress. It was shown too on my last journey to the Far East when I attended a conference of Foreign Operations Administration Mission Directors from the Philippines, Formosa, Thailand, Burma, Indonesia, the Associated States of Indo-China, by the United Nations Economic Coordinator for Korea and a State Department representative to Japan. I was enormously impressed by the progress of our projects in this region and I saw for myself the beginnings of local light industry for the production of consumer goods, improved working conditions, substantial increase in the real wages of the workers, and the beneficial results of modern irrigation and improved crop methods.

For the first time since World War II the supply of food in non-Communist Asia is adequate. In some areas good crop years have enabled people to accumulate supplies of rice for emergency purposes. However, there is the resultant problem of inadequate transportation, of blocked-up trade routes, of a trickle of commodities flowing between communities and countries where there could and should be a swift-moving stream. For the most part populations are congested, disease is rampant, and the standards of living are pitifully low. We recognize the urgency of these problems from the standpoint of our own national security and with the welfare of our friends in Asia in mind, we are doing something about them.

In 1952, for example, only 12 per cent of total mutual security funds were devoted to the Far East and the Pacific. Under current mutual security programs it is expected that 53 per cent will flow to this region. This is a positive response to the genuine needs of our Asian partners.

Even though the unfolding pattern in Asia might appear, on the surface, to be similar to the problems confronted in Europe after World War II, it is important that we understand and consider the patent difference that exists.

In the first place, the approach in Asia must be viewed with a long-range perspective. It is one thing to set out in Europe to restore what *once was,* with the work accelerated by an abundance of already available technical competence. It is another thing to build in Asia what *never was* and under the handicap of scant technical know-how.

The problems in Asia are complex and many. Their ultimate solution depends first on the initiative of the Asian people themselves and second, on the degree to which a concerted and common plan of action can be organized by the industrially developed nations. It is my earnest hope that those countries of Western Europe whose rapid recovery was effectively helped by the Marshall Plan concept will see their way to joining the United States in creating a clearing house of cooperation between the developed and less advanced nations. Only in this way, with carefully thought-out plans, numbered not in months but in years, can the free world create a better tomorrow and help all people to make a decent living and a decent life.

Let me add that if, by encouraging self-help, we are carrying on clearly humanitarian programs, they are just as obviously the product of hard-headed thinking. In the lesser developed areas of the world lie our life-lines with vital raw material sources. Ninety per cent of our manganese needed in the production of steel, all of our supply of new tin, two thirds of our aluminum-containing ores, most of our uranium ore, and in all about 75 per cent of our strategic raw materials are supplied by the less developed countries of the world.

From another viewpoint there is a clear and urgent need to create new and broader markets to nurture our constantly expanding industrial machine.

Let me cite some revealing figures. The United States, containing six per cent of the world's population, accounts for about

40 per cent of the world's goods and services. The countries of free Asia, comprising about one third of the world's peoples, produces about 8 per cent of the world's goods and services. The United States and the free world's other industrial nations, despite a relatively high level of consumption at home, require ever-expanding markets abroad, to assure prosperity. In the presently underdeveloped countries lies a vast potential and a mutuality of interest. As these countries develop, as we help them to develop, their economic advance, their rising standard of living will create new markets for the industrial nations of the world, including the United States. This is the route to mutual strength, mutual progress, and mutual security.

"OPERATION RATHOLE" [2]

I call foreign aid "Operation Rathole."

Since 1948 Congress has appropriated $45.3 billion for foreign nations around the world.

This year Congress is being asked to appropriate an additional $3.5 billion for the same purpose.

If Congress did not appropriate a penny of this new money, the Foreign Operations Administration (FOA) would still have $7.9 billion to dole out as it chooses to foreign governments. In other words, Congress has been asked and is being asked to vote funds for foreign countries faster than a succession of foreign aid agencies can find places and ways to spend it.

Foreign aid expenditures during fiscal 1956 are scheduled to total $4.7 billion. This is $400 million more than last year. Obviously with $3.5 billion asked, the FOA plans to use up some of this carry-over money, but by no means all.

At the current rate of foreign aid expenditures, the foreign aid program could be continued for two more years without Congress' voting any amount at all.

[2] From "Should U.S. Aid Other Countries?" article by Senator George W. Malone (Republican, Nevada). *Foreign Policy Bulletin*. 34:117. April 15, 1955. Reprinted by permission.

Three and a half billion dollars saved would enable my party to meet its campaign commitments of balancing the budget. Instead, the Administration is predicting a $2.4 billion deficit.

A $3.5 billion saving would make possible the $20 tax deduction for every American citizen that the Administration very recently so bitterly opposed. Or it would enable the excise-tax and corporation-tax reductions, which originally were scheduled to take place April 1, to go into effect without increasing the total budget or the anticipated deficit.

Foreign aid since World War II has been a device to tap the taxpayers, maintain a large and growing government payroll here and abroad, and build up industries in foreign countries with low wage scales to compete against our own markets.

Article I, Section 8, of the United States Constitution states that Congress shall have power to lay and collect taxes to pay the debts and "provide for the common defense and general welfare of the United States." Nowhere does it grant Congress the power to lay and collect taxes to provide for the defense of Europe or Europe's general welfare. Yet that is where $45.3 billion in taxes collected from the American people has gone, and where it is proposed to send billions more.

As to payment of the debts of the United States, those debts have increased $11 billion since we began doling out wealth to foreign nations. We now have not only the largest public debt in our history but the largest of any nation in the history of the world.

During this period when we have been building up the competitive economies of foreign nations with billions in foreign aid, the number of distressed areas and communities here has increased tremendously.

Two years ago there were 37 such areas; a year ago, 51; and today there are 144. Congress has never been asked to vote a penny to aid these areas and the American citizens within these areas.

Surplus food was distributed to approximately two million American citizens in the last half of 1954, but that already has been paid for by the taxpayers. Food doles averaged twenty-four pounds per person.

The manufacture of textiles was the dominant industry in twenty of these distressed areas—the areas and industry stricken by textile imports from nations to which we have extended millions or billions in foreign aid. Textiles also ranked as the second or third most important industry in six other areas.

Mining was the dominant industry in 33 distressed areas and a major industry in 5 others; lumber, a major industry in 7; leather, in 4; glass, in 4; metals, in 14; and electrical machinery, in 17. Import competition from aided countries contributed to the economic distress of these American industries.

Foreign aid is a one-way street, all outgo.

In return for our largess 69 foreign countries apply import licenses against goods of United States origin and 48 require exchange permits before their nationals can pay for American goods. Thirty-two nations have raised tariffs on goods imported from the United States. Still we pour out aid. Every European country to which we have given aid has expanded its industrial production 30 to 80 per cent above its prewar high.

Meanwhile, in the United States we have 3.75 million unemployed, a growing public debt, a continued treasury deficit, and a perpetuation of high wartime corporation and excise taxes.

IT IS NOT "DOWN THE DRAIN" [3]

The . . . debate over economic aid to Asia is surely one of the most curiously muffled political controversies of recent years. . . .

The reason for this confusion seems fairly straightforward. "Economic aid" has become in the eyes of many politicians a thoroughly bad business. They equate it with all the different ways in which foreigners are supposed to make a sucker of Uncle Sam. It is "global boondoggling." It is pouring billions down the drain. It is sending good money after bad and the voters won't stand for it.

[3] From article by Barbara Ward, British writer and editor on foreign and economic affairs. New York *Times Magazine.* p9+. March 13, 1955. Reprinted by permission.

Military aid, it is true, seems to have none of these over-tones. Military weapons have a blessedly concrete appearance. They can be compared with the pictures of Red armaments lined up in Moscow and Peiping, and strength is matched against strength. The appearance is all of value being had for the money.

But a picture, say, of peasants receiving a distribution of improved seed has a look on it of charity and the handout. Little about it conveys the possibility that before the next harvest the whole bunch of peasants might have gone off and become Communist guerrillas out of sheer discouragement. Military aid, in short, barely has to argue the case for itself. Economic aid is guilty until proved innocent—and possibly even then.

It is not difficult to state the rational argument against such an attitude. An arms program that is not backed by economic strength is like a boxer with a big punch and a weak heart. The first battles turn upon weapons, the last upon the state of the economy—as the Russians learned in 1917 or the Germans after 1942. This need for economic staying power is particularly and obviously urgent in any long contest with Communists since they rely to such an extent upon subversion and infiltration.

The argument is not abstract. A few years ago, three quarters of all American aid was directed to Europe. Since the end of the Marshall Plan in 1952 and the highly successful completion of its work of economic reconstruction, it has proved possible so to switch military and economic aid that three quarters of it can go to Asia. Economic aid has been a means of putting Europe in a better military posture. Moreover, it has made possible the large British and Commonwealth contribution to economic aid in Asia, which, under the Colombo Plan, has been running at over $750 million a year. [See "Using the Colombo Plan" in this section below.]

A more recent example from Asia is quite as striking. The Communists gained their great influence over the Telegu-speaking peoples around Madras, in India, during the famine years of 1951-52. They were behind the agitation to secure a separate linguistic state for the Telegu-speakers—the state of Andhra—

which they believed they would dominate, thus creating a first large Communist enclave in the Indian Union.

But in the intervening years the Indian Government has been able to overcome the food shortage. Two good monsoons aided them, but the turning point was the American wheat loan, which staved off starvation during the actual famine and afterward provided the grain reserves which, in the last three years, have been used to put an end to hoarding—a particular grievance around Madras and one eagerly exploited by the Communists. When elections came in Andhra recently, the Communists were —to their own intense astonishment—completely routed. In short, the contribution made earlier in economic aid has proved a vital factor in preventing the establishment of a new Communist bridgehead in Asia.

Such arguments, however, do not convince a politician whose attitude toward economic aid is based on the belief that "the voters won't stand for it." He has it in his mind that while the man in the street can see the logic of weapons and the necessity of making them available to threatened nations, the whole business of economic aid appears wasteful and ineffective and bound up with ideas of idle foreigners getting something for nothing and then not even showing decent human gratitude for what has been done.

Admittedly, this may be the attitude of some citizens, but anyone who has traveled widely and recently in the United States cannot but conduct his or her own poll on the matter, and one traveler at least has been driven to wonder whether this picture of an American public opinion acquiescent where military aid is concerned but highly suspicious of any economic measures of assistance may not be very wide of the mark.

In the first place, now that the chief military instrument behind diplomacy is the hydrogen bomb, people are bound to question its appropriateness. The groundswell of neutralism and pacifism in European and Asian politics is no doubt stronger than any comparable sentiment in America, for Britain or Germany or Burma or India feel themselves at once more exposed to attack and less in control of policy than does the United States. Yet there can be no doubt of the deep emotional support given by Americans to President Eisenhower's repeated denunciation of war, to his pleas for patience and negotiation and utter rejection of "aggression" over the Chinese mainland or anywhere else. . . .

Among more reflective groups, one should also record an opposite, though related, reason for uneasiness over the primacy given to military and strategic needs. The question is whether the hydrogen bomb may not have produced a stalemate, in which neither side dare use their ultimate military weapons—the situation described by Sir Winston Churchill in which survival will be "twin brother of annihilation." In that event, the main risk to security might come from the small wars of the world—civil wars, local struggles fomented from abroad, or frontier clashes magnified by outside support.

In such disputes, notoriously, the entry points for trouble are often provided by local discontent, peasant dissatisfaction, the disintegration of tribal or traditional society—in a word, by a variety of social and economic upheavals not all of them amenable to military action, yet offering some scope to a diplomacy which has not emptied all economic instruments out of its locker. If the world is to be dominated by thermonuclear stalemate, some people are asking whether economic aid may not in fact be a primary military necessity.

But it would not be accurate to ascribe all evidence of new attitudes simply to changes in strategic ideas or to negative fears of atomic destruction. From journeys, which in the last year have extended to most sections of the United States, the writer must record the impression that positive interest in foreign peoples and even a sense of concern for their progress and welfare is at least as prevalent as the opposite attitude of distrust and dislike. . . .

What a paradox appears, therefore, to underlie American or indeed Western diplomacy today! Under pressure of a supposed public opinion, it has, in recent years, attempted to do more and more of its good, as it were, by stealth. Economic aid has been increasingly hidden behind the screen of military aid, or allowed to drop. . . .

In the East, . . . the military preparedness of Japan has taken priority of attention over the earlier approach of economic aid. Such military pacts as that with Pakistan have overshadowed the continuance of economic aid to India. Southeast Asia Treaty Organization had yet to implement any sort of economic program. Today, the whole debate over economic aid for Asia is so confused that many people, both inside and outside America, have the impression that economic aid is virtually a thing of the past.

Needless to say, such beliefs have proved invaluable to Communist propaganda everywhere. After the paralyzing setback of the Marshall Plan, Communists have returned delightedly to the theme of America as a selfish, capitalist bloodsucker, exploiting its own and other peoples and disgorging none of the wealth it has wrung from their labors. On the contrary, in the Communist picture, it uses its wealth to prepare for war and to spread aggression through the world. Unhappily, every time Western economic aid is hidden beneath a military cloak, the effectiveness of these themes is multiplied a hundredfold.

The trend is all the more disconcerting in that, in effect, generous aid programs have been carried on. More than a billion dollars has been spent by Americans in the last twelve months and about three quarters of that figure by the British Commonwealth. But much of their impact has been weakened, their effect minimized by the Communists' ability to quote Western sources on the necessity to end economic aid and to do so fast. . . .

Those who seek to smother economic aid under military covers—or attempt to do away with it altogether—are not only mistaken in their estimate of the relative effectiveness of the two forms of aid. They are almost certainly wrong in their gauging of public opinion. Vigorous and articulate leadership in support of economic aid at this time and during the coming Asian debate could, therefore, have the effect not only of regaining the initiative from the Communists on the world front of words. It could help to restore a sense of hope and direction to a bemused and apprehensive public opinion at home.

USING THE COLOMBO PLAN [4]

Considerations of both politics and economics . . . lead us inevitably to the same conclusion: A vigorous program of economic assistance to Asia should be at the core of United States foreign policy.

How can the program be carried out? A new and hopeful means is now available to us. The Colombo Plan, which was originally a family affair within the British Commonwealth, has now been expanded to take in practically all of non-Communist Asia. [The Colombo Plan grew out of a meeting of British Commonwealth prime ministers at Colombo, capital of Ceylon, in January 1950. Non-Commonwealth countries such as Burma and Indonesia were invited to join from the very beginning. The idea was to plan the economic development of South and Southeast Asia on a regional level, discussing the needs and priorities of the undeveloped countries and the possibilities of aid from Britain and other dominions capable of furnishing assistance. The plan was officially initiated on July 1, 1951. The United States has been a member of the plan's consultative committee since 1951 but has carried on its Asian aid programs on a bilateral basis with the plan's member countries. Membership now blankets most of free Asia, with Thailand, the Philippines and Japan joining in 1954.

[The Colombo Plan should not be confused with references to "the Colombo powers." The latter is an informal grouping so named because the prime ministers of India, Pakistan, Ceylon, Indonesia and Burma met at the Ceylonese capital in 1954. The main emphasis of their grouping is political rather than economic.—Ed.]

The Colombo Plan has now become the center where a dozen national-development plans are synchronized. What's more, it allows western nations to help Asians without arousing their suspicions. The Asians themselves are spending about $2 billion this year on the Colombo Plan, and loans and grants from the

[4] From "The Job Harold Stassen Leaves Unfinished," article by Representative Harrison A. Williams (Democrat, New Jersey). *Reporter.* 12:32-3. April 7, 1955. Reprinted by permission.

United States, Britain, Canada, Australia, and New Zealand have amounted to $1 billion since 1950. Alongside this investment program there is a thriving program of technical assistance: Five thousand Asians are being trained, and twenty-five hundred British and Commonwealth experts are building dams, making geological surveys, and applying the West's skills to the East's problems in a hundred fields.

This existing association of Asian nations could be expanded into a source of investment capital for the entire region with the backing of United States funds. A unilateral United States' program might be called imperialism; a multilateral program under United Nations auspices might be sabotaged by Soviet participation. The Colombo Plan avoids both dangers.

What's keeping us from doing what obviously needs to be done in Asia? . . . One obstacle is our own fixed prejudices about foreign investment. . . .

The illusion persists in the present as well as in the previous Administration that private investors can meet most of the need for capital in the economically underdeveloped areas of the world. It is an attractive idea, but the simple truth is that right here at home, to say nothing of prospering Canada, the investor finds more lucrative and far safer investment opportunities than are to be found in any underdeveloped area. Foreign countries are now paying us half again as much return on past investments as American citizens are currently investing abroad. I am afraid that continued efforts by the government to entice American investors abroad will have little effect. Private investors will go into the less developed areas only after some advance has been made on the basic problems of transportation, communication, and health. This can only be done by some form of public investment.

The International Bank for Reconstruction and Development does part of this job—the part that a strictly banking operation can appropriately do. The Export-Import Bank exists to promote United States trade rather than investment in other countries; so it too can meet only a limited need on a limited scale.

The proposed International Finance Corporation would be an excellent further step in the right direction. By investing in enterprises that Asians themselves start and manage and then selling off its holdings locally when the enterprises become profitable, such a corporation could promote industrial development and help to create a capital market at the same time. It would, however, leave still unsolved the problem of where the money for basic economic development is to come from.

For too many years, our government has suffered from a lack of imagination in grappling with the whole problem of public investment in less developed areas. Only two forms of assistance have generally been thought feasible: direct grants, which are onerous to the recipients as well as to United States taxpayers; and dollar loans that have to be repaid directly in dollars.

And yet there are other forms of dollar assistance that could be used. We need to learn to use them in Asia.

Suppose we should adopt a program to help finance a regional-development bank under the Colombo Plan. The United States could provide the bank with a major share of its initial capital, and loans to the participating countries could then be paid back to the regional bank in local currency. This money could then be loaned out again for further development projects. Such a scheme would have several advantages:

It would create a long-term revolving fund to meet the need for continuous investment in such fields as public health, education, agriculture, and communications.

It would avoid the difficulty of repayment in dollars.

It would avoid the onus of "charity" for the recipient and some of the equally onerous "giveaway" implications for United States taxpayers.

It would clearly indicate a permanent interest on our part in helping Asians to realize their economic aspirations.

WORDS, DOLLARS AND POWER [5]

Today, Eastern Asia, aside from a few islands of American semi-control—Japan, Formosa and the Philippines—is almost a closed continent to American influence. We have not won

[5] From *Billions, Blunders and Baloney* by Eugene W. Castle, film editor, distributor, and producer. Devin-Adair Company. New York. 1955. p 196-7, 201-3 and 205-6. Reprinted by permission.

Asiatic friendship through our sleek, streamlined propaganda plays; we have acquired smoldering, unappeasable Asiatic hate. Through vast stretches of the Asiatic continent, the United States today has scarcely an admitted friend. . . .

In retrospect, it is now easy to perceive that our information and aid agencies have never understood the task of combating communism in East Asia. Two main points of view have guided postwar Americans in Asia. Both have been dangerously wrong.

The first is the do-gooder point of view which has conceived the Asia job as one of bringing sanitation, good diet, American technical skills, and, particularly, American democracy to East Asians. The earliest exponent of this school was the forgotten Henry A. Wallace. Its present loudest voice is that of Chester Bowles, Truman Ambassador to India. Mr. Bowles would have drenched the Indians with American generosity. He proposed in 1952 that we award a billion-dollar relief program to India, spaced out over four years, to finance Nehru's Five Year Plan. Trusting in Nehru's good faith with the United States, Bowles would build an American Asiatic policy on the weak reed of a quixotic Nehruism.

Bowles's trustful proposals were knocked into a cocked hat by Congress, and Bowles himself soon made his departure, but the mawkish, over-sentimental attitude which he symbolizes is still widespread among American information, aid and Technical Cooperation Administration workers in Asia. Not understanding the Asiatic mind, such do-gooders imagine that a weak American humanitarianism can stand up against the magnetic promise of "Asia for the Asiatics" which the Communists have shrewdly inherited from the war-time Japanese. All that the Bowleses accomplish is a complete loss of face by Americans among Asiatics. The postwar Asiatic is not receptive to "Big Brothers" from the West. He wants to expel the West and do the reforming, if he does it, in his own way and time.

The second American approach which has been tried and which has failed in Asia, is the "buy friendship" approach. Those who follow this line are not ideologues like the Bowleses, but they are equally mistaken. Their method is that of the political broker. They hope to exchange so many American millions (or billions) for a corresponding reward of Asiatic good-will. Most of the Mutual Security Administration disbursement functionaries are of this mind.

Harold Stassen has now revealed that the Administration has decided to place all its chips in the Far East upon this bankrupt "buy friends" policy.

In a full-dress news conference on November 22, 1954, Mr. Stassen impressively announced that a new Marshall Plan for Asia was to be the next major undertaking of the Administration. . . .

The viciousness of this new proposal is that it contradicts President Eisenhower's own words, in his speech before the nation's editors on June 23, 1954, when the President declared that "you cannot keep any other country in the world free merely by money." The President wisely added on this occasion that "you can't buy or import a heart or a soul, or a determination to remain free."

And yet, Mr. Stassen has officially announced that the Administration has decided to go all-out for a program which, not many months ago, the President himself declared to be impossible.

Anyone even remotely familiar with Asiatic realities realizes the ineffable folly of such a project. . . . Asia will avidly take the money but, for the most part, will remain neutralist toward primary American objectives in the West Pacific. . . .

The only American method which has a ghost of a chance of winning Asiatics, according to one school of thought, is the one worked out by General Douglas MacArthur in Japan during the years of his supreme command. It is the method of controlled, even-handed power. It is the method of gradualistic betterment of social and economic conditions balanced by a scrupulous respect for Asiatic sensibilities and folkways. It is the method of undeviating support of America's Asiatic friends and ruthless firmness in dealing with America's enemies or challengers. It is the method of the all-out, instead of the method of the half-hearted. It is a method, however, that would require the consent of Congress, backed by the majority of American opinion; a method that heretofore in our history we have not looked upon with favor.

Asiatics instinctively respect power. They respect realistic, practical approaches by the West. They have no hooks in their minds upon which to hang the mealy-mouthed preachments of the "One World" impossibilists whom we have sent among them. With their rooted traditions, they can have nothing but contempt for a Washington which fires a Douglas MacArthur and sends them a Chester Bowles. . . .

America has the power, but some failure of will stops it from exercising that power in the psychological moments when it could enforce its objectives. With the steady onrush of the Soviets, America's opportunities are narrowing. Possibly the usual American method of using words and dollars is nearing its inevitable and ineffectual conclusion.

INVESTMENT IN STRENGTH [6]

It has been suggested on occasion that our superiority in modern weapons has lessened our need for allied support. This is a dangerous misconception. We need the support of other free nations just as they need us. The peoples of these nations, their territories, their farms and factories, their mines and scientific and technical skills, all are priceless assets in the hands of the free. But under Communist control these human and material resources would be harnessed and used against us.

I have repeatedly emphasized the fact that we cannot rely exclusively upon any single weapon or technique; that our technological advantages must be reinforced by other means of defense, both military and nonmilitary. Superiority in modern weapons is not a product of any special magic, nor is it auto-

[6] From "The Mutual Security Program—An Investment in Strength," statement by John Foster Dulles, Secretary of State, before the Senate Foreign Relations Committee, May 5, 1955. *United States Department of State Bulletin.* 32:856. May 23, 1955.

matically guaranteed to last forever. It is part of our over-all technological capacity and is a composite of various human skills, mineral resources, laboratories and factories, trained military personnel, bases, and other facilities, many of which are freely made available by our friends and allies. Technological superiority for a prolonged period will depend in large measure upon what happens to people in other lands and upon how they decide to use their human and physical resources.

There are some who have criticized the Mutual Security Program as a futile effort to buy friendship. If this were its true purpose, it would indeed be futile. Friendship cannot be purchased. The great majority of the free peoples of the world are already friendly to the United States. Our real purpose is to invest in strength. We want to make our friends as strong as possible, so that they can better protect themselves and contribute more effectively to our common safety and to our common progress toward a more stable and peaceful world.

During the past ten years the free nations have voluntarily forged a partnership relationship which has served them well. The United States has made a momentous contribution to that partnership. Never for a moment have we sought aggrandizement for ourselves. Our only purpose has been to help those elsewhere who believed in human freedom and were willing themselves to struggle and sacrifice to assure it. What the American people have done over this ten-year period has, I think, no precedent in recorded history.

What has been done warrants good hopes for the future. Those hopes are primarily due to the fact that men are now realizing that peace and justice are goals which must be constantly worked for and sacrificed for and that they are not goals which can be assured by some paper agreement or by some sporadic act. In the past, almost always, war has led to agreements which people interpreted as assuring peace. Therefore, they relaxed and went about their purely personal affairs. This time we have not relaxed but have gone on working and struggling—sometimes with success, sometimes with setbacks, but always with determination.

ONE MAN'S ASIAN REVOLUTION [7]

In a remote Philippine village, many miles from Manila, I
saw recently a crude hand-lettered poster hanging in a palm-
thatched shed. It read:

Go to the People.
Live among them.
Learn from them.
Love them.
Serve them.
Plan with them.
Start with what they know.
Build on what they have.

Reading it, my thoughts went back twenty years—to another
such primitive village, in China, where "Jimmy" Yen had set up
a "social and human laboratory" to teach the long-ignored peasants how to fight poverty, ignorance and disease. For, as the
poster proclaimed, this Filipino village, too, was now under the
spell of Jimmy's zeal and genius.

What Jimmy Yen had learned in thirty years of social crusad-
ing in his native land is today being successfully applied in the
Philippines. With the enthusiastic backing of President Ramón
Magsaysay, that country has become the pilot plant for an idea
which, if it fulfills its present promise, may hold the best hope
for keeping free Asia free. For basically the problems of the
masses throughout the East are the same. They long desperately
for two things: a full rice bowl and human dignity. And no one
is more searchingly aware than Jimmy Yen that these are the
best antidotes to communism.

Long before there was Point Four, there was Yen. Dr. Y. C.
Yen, a lean, wise, dedicated scholar who looks far younger than
his sixty years, is world-famous for the Mass Education Movement he launched in China shortly after World War I. In the
years before the Chinese Red Government made it impossible for

[7] From "Jimmy Yen and the People's Crusade," article by J. P. McEvoy,
Reader's Digest roving editor. *Reader's Digest*. 66:142-52. March 1955. Reprinted by permission.

him to work there, Jimmy Yen taught millions of illiterate Chinese peasants how to read, how to make better livings, how to improve their health—in short, how to live. . . .

Jimmy Yen first came to know the needs of Asia's humble people in—of all places—France. In World War I, 200,000 Chinese coolies had been brought to Europe to work behind the Allied lines. Jimmy, whose family had been scholars for generations, was one of those American-educated Chinese who volunteered to go overseas to supervise and help. What followed has become a classic of adult education.

One day a coolie begged Jimmy to write a letter to his wife in China. Next day the man returned with two others. Soon Jimmy's days and nights were crowded with writing letters and reading replies. Studying these letters, he made a stunning discovery: of the forty thousand written Chinese characters, only a handful were needed to communicate the coolies' fears, hopes and simple wants. Jimmy boiled these characters down to about a thousand and asked for volunteers to learn them.

At first the men were incredulous. A peasant learning to read and write? In four thousand years of Chinese history, no one had heard of such a thing. Finally, out of five thousand present at a mass meeting, forty daring souls volunteered.

"After four months of teaching, thirty-five graduated," Yen recalls. "They stood up before the camp and proudly read news bulletins chalked on a blackboard. The others looked as though they were seeing a miracle. And they were!"

Jimmy reasoned that if forty illiterates could learn to read by his method, so could the rest of the 200,000. Using his first class as a pilot group—a technique he has followed ever since— he made the brightest of them "assistant teachers" to train others. At the same time he taught his method to some eighty colleagues in charge of other camps. "The Miracle of the Thousand Characters" repeated itself over and over. . . .

Dr. Yen returned to China in 1920 fired with a great mission. He would teach his country's illiterate millions to read and write. . . .

His Mass Education Movement spread rapidly. . . . Millions of peasants, old and young, learned to read. But what would they read, and who was going to write it? In four thousand years nobody had seemed to care what the submerged 85 per cent of China's population wanted or needed. He had run into a situation which is still a curse throughout Asia.

Recently Yen traveled through Indonesia, India, Pakistan, Thailand, as well as the Philippines. He says, "The urgent need in all these countries is a new literature adapted to the new literate masses. In one country I was told that 25 per cent of the people now could read. The plan, an education department official told me, is to wipe out illiteracy in ten years. 'That's wonderful,' I said. 'What literature have you prepared for people with a very limited vocabulary? Is anybody providing vital, appealing reading matter?' 'Yes—the Communists,' the official said sadly."

In China Dr. Yen had to begin "a long and painful process of re-educating the educated" to prepare a new form of literature for the masses. Eventually he and his scholar-colleagues produced a "people's library" of a thousand booklets in basic Chinese, ranging from the classics, folk tales and songs to modern farming, rural hygiene, cooperatives.

"Once a man's mind is stimulated by reading," Yen explains, "you've started something you can't stop. He wants also to learn how to live. But to teach peasants we should know how peasants live. Since eight out of ten Chinese are in the villages, that is where we went."

Thus was born the celebrated "laboratory" at Tinghsien in north China, a typical *hsien* (county) of mud villages about a day's journey from Peiping. It was here I first met Jimmy Yen more than twenty years ago. I can still see his blazing black eyes, his slender, wiry body that vibrated like a tuning fork as he preached his gospel. Even to this day Jimmy never talks —he exhorts.

I shall never forget the little children who came to the Tinghsien school just long enough to learn the five characters which the teacher had written on the blackboard. Once they could read and write these characters the bell rang and they scattered in all directions. I followed a small girl to her rendezvous, under a tree, with a group of tiny children. Their new

teacher, with great authority, traced in the dust the five characters she had just learned, and her pupils traced them after her.
This proud little schoolmarm could hardly contain herself long
enough to pass on what she knew so she could hurry back to
learn some more. . . .

What has Jimmy Yen used for money all these thirty-odd
years? . . .

During the initial years, when the major emphasis was upon
literacy, Yen did not need much money. There were literally
thousands of volunteer teachers and workers. But in 1928, when
emphasis was shifted to rural reconstruction, American friends
advised him to go to the United States to enlist support. Henry
Ford contributed $10,000. He said, "Mr. Yen, I like your idea.
You go about mass educating people the way I go about mass
producing cars." . . .

On that first American tour Jimmy raised half a million
dollars for the Mass Education Movement. This money directly
benefited some 400,000 people in the Tinghsien area. More
important, that training center radiated its influence all over
China, so that in 1937 when the Japanese invaded, there were
800 such centers. By then Yen was ready to operate on a China-
wide scale, but the Japanese had other ideas.

Even during the war, however, his pioneers kept going.
When there was fighting in the North, they worked in the South.
When the fighting was in the South, they worked in the
West. . . .

After V-J Day, Dr. Yen set the reconstruction of the rural
population of the entire country as his goal. . . . He carried
his battle to America, this time in a campaign for millions of
dollars. The United States had poured millions into China, but
how much of it had ever gotten down to the people for what
they needed and wanted? With the aid of American friends he
tackled Congress, which appointed a committee to draft a bill
for the Yen Plan. . . . The China Aid Act of 1948 allocated
$27 million solely to rural reconstruction, in a section of the Act
which came to be known as "The Jimmy Yen Provision." . . .

When China fell, the Yen program had improved life for
an estimated sixty million peasants at a total outlay of about five

million dollars; it was the most successful American aid program ever undertaken. And it is being continued today on Formosa, with remarkable results in rice production, rural health and, especially, in land reform.

After the fall of China, Jimmy Yen's life's work was seemingly in ruins. But he wasn't giving up. The lessons of three decades of pioneering were available to what remained of free Asia. . . . Jimmy and his friends formed an International Committee of the Mass Education Movement, to promote rural reconstruction in countries that ask for it. With its backing, he made an exploratory trip, early in 1952, to the Philippines, Thailand, Indonesia, India and Pakistan.

Upon his return he reported [that] . . . the four basic problems of peasants everywhere . . . are the same: poverty, ignorance, disease and misgovernment. These problems interlock; the solution of one depends upon the successful solution of the others. The real need, therefore, is for an integrated, rounded-out program.

"It would be wonderful," Yen concluded, "if we could pick out one country as an all-out testing ground. Just as farmers need a demonstration farm, so the nations need a demonstration nation."

Did he have a particular country in mind? "Yes, the Philippines," he said. "Its problems are typical of Asia as a whole. Because it is not too large, striking results can be produced quickly—and we are racing against time." . . .

Thus, under Jimmy Yen's leadership, the Philippine Rural Reconstruction Movement was born. . . .

What is the Yen Plan? Its key word is "human mobilization" —mobilizing, training and organizing the village adults, youths and children. The goal, when the job is done, is not only new villages but a new people, with new habits, skills, mentality and a new spirit. Rural reconstruction means "human reconstruction." The secret of its success is fourfold:

First, it is economical, saving not only money but time. Trained Filipino volunteer workers live with the people and use their help and materials to work out immediate economic, social and political reforms.

Second, its techniques are simple to learn and simple to teach. It begins with what the peasant has and knows, and it helps him to build step by step.

Third, it is fundamental. Health and hygiene begin with the sanitary privy. Education begins with learning to read and write. The villagers are shown how to raise better crops; how to organize buying and selling coöperatives; how to lift the age-old curse of predatory landlords and crushing interest charges by forming credit unions. They learn true self-government by actually running their own affairs.

Fourth, the Yen Plan is self-duplicating. A model center multiplies into a model community which in turn becomes a pilot plant, a demonstration station and a training school for enthusiasts who then spread out to other regions and repeat their successes.

I saw this Yen Plan under way in more than a hundred Filipino villages. Already the influence of the Movement has spread to two thousand villages, and this is only the beginning. . . .

In the villages you can see, as I did, the physical conversion of tumbledown huts into neat, clean homes; wretched diseased villages into model healthy communities; filthy back yards into fenced poultry-runs and gardens. More important, you can see an amazing job of human reconstruction—peasants in adult-literacy schools; cottage-industry classes; health clinics run by newly trained laymen; the transformation of remote, destitute apathetic rural masses into ambitious, civic-minded citizens proud of their accomplishments and eager to learn more.

More thrilling even than the awakened adults are the youthful volunteers—high school and college graduates, trained to help these peasants help themselves. With the vigorous idealism of youth, they live with the people, share their meager fare and work around the clock. These are the kind of young people the Communists go after first in every country, but Jimmy Yen has inspired them with his own zeal for our brand of democracy. . . .

Given the needed help, the Philippines can become the "demonstration nation" envisioned by Dr. Yen, to prove that economic sufficiency and political democracy can be achieved on Asian soil by an Asian people.

"Revolution of the first magnitude, economic as well as political, is on the move throughout Asia today," Dr. Yen says. "The masses are clamoring for a better life. Ideologies or isms do not interest them. What they want is the full rice bowl and human dignity. Whichever side will help them realize their simple aspirations will win the day."

That's the challenge and the hope. The Philippines, and Jimmy Yen's people's crusade, are showing a way to all of Asia.

IV. ARMS AND IDEAS

EDITOR'S INTRODUCTION

After the experience of the Korean war, most Americans agree that the United States and its Asian allies should remain prepared in the event that Communist military aggression strikes again. A more difficult problem—and one that brings conflicting opinions—is posed by situations such as that faced by the French in Indo-China. How do we combat the combination of guerrilla and political warfare that the Communists seem so adept at waging?

If we could find the answer to this question, it would help us to synthesize all three arms of our foreign policy—economic, military and political. If we could help Asians to see the perils of Communist totalitarianism, if we could help them see the advantages and vast potentials of democratic freedom, then we would be reasonably sure that our military and economic aims would be accomplished.

The following articles give a number of points of view—sometimes divergent, sometimes complementary—on these questions. The first three articles emphasize the need for military strength. The authors that follow tend to stress the problem of giving Asians the will to resist communism and to build and defend their own democratic ways of life.

THE MILITARY AID PROGRAM [1]

The military aid program is part and parcel of the United States Defense Department program. The expenditures abroad

[1] From a statement by Admiral Arthur Radford, chairman of the Joint Chiefs of Staff before the Senate Foreign Relations Committee, May 9, 1955. In *Mutual Security Act of 1955;* hearings before the Committee on Foreign Relations, United States, 84th Congress, 1st session, on the mutual security program for fiscal year 1956. May 5-23, 1955. The Committee. Washington, D.C. 1955. p97-100.

in support of our alliances do not differ in purpose, scope, or objective from our own military expenditures. The fact that this part of our program is not included in the Defense Department budget is more a matter of procedure and administration than of substance. In this connection I can assure you that were it not for the strength which has been generated in the past five years by our allies—and in most instances made possible by our military aid programs—the requirements of our own program would be much larger.

Our security today is inextricably bound with that of the other nations of the free world. Our plans and programs must be worked out in cooperation with our allies in order to obtain maximum effectiveness in the development and employment of forces and facilities. In this mutual effort, each ally should play a part commensurate with its capabilities.

Although we have spent a great deal of money on our military assistance programs they have paid large dividends and will continue to do so. These programs have resulted not only in greatly improved collective strength, but they have made it possible for the individual countries of the free world to concentrate on the development of those forces which constitute their most effective contribution to the whole. Together these nations provide a pool of collective strength. If we are to be adequately prepared and simultaneously maintain a stable economy for the long pull, our forces must generally complement each other and constitute balanced forces on a global scale.

This balance can best be attained by each nation contributing to the pool those forces and facilities that it is most proficient and best capable of developing. In view of our vast industrial capacity, technological ability and limited manpower, we believe that the most effective contribution which the United States is capable of making consists of complex technical weapons and equipment, modern air and naval power, and highly mobile offensive combat forces backed up by ready reserves. On the other hand, we feel that the other allied nations can most efficiently provide in their own and adjacent countries the bulk of the defensive ground forces and local naval and air power.

It would be a dangerous misconception to assume that our superiority in modern weapons has reduced our need for allies. In my opinion, the free nations' coalition can ill afford to let the Iron Curtain ring down on additional countries of the free world. Though it often seems unclear, and is sometimes deliberately obscured, Communist domination means that more resources will be harnessed to their war machine and may be turned against us. Every resource added to the Communist bloc constitutes a subtraction from the total of the free world. In effect, the relative gain is therefore double the apparent gain. If communism is permitted to gobble up parts of the world one by one, the day could come when the Communist bloc would be so powerful that no corner of the world would be safe.

It is virtually impossible for many of the nations of the free world to maintain and equip sizable forces without our assistance. The Republic of Korea and the Republic of China are two outstanding examples. Today the Republic of Korea has twenty-one ground divisions on active duty. The forces of the Republic of China are significant in numbers and have been steadily strengthened since 1951. These troops are well equipped and highly trained. Combined with the mobile forces which we can contribute they constitute together a bulwark of strength on the side of the free world in the western Pacific.

Furthermore, the generation and maintenance of this allied strength has permitted the United States to redeploy ground divisions from that area and to reduce the total number of troops that we must maintain on active duty. It has permitted us to concentrate on the development of those complex weapons, equipment and forces which we are more proficient in developing than are many of our allies. This is an example of balanced forces on a global scale.

Thus you can see that the mutual defense assistance program is an integral part of our own national security program. It is designed to generate essential military strength in the free world which is complemented by our own national forces. Such a program can hardly be labeled a giveaway program. On the contrary it is an essential and realistic one from our standpoint. One basic fact which cannot be disregarded is that the United

States alone does not have available, nor could we maintain on active duty for an indefinite period, the forces necessary to match the Communist bloc in manpower at every possible point of aggression around the globe. We need each and every one of our allies and they need us if we are to maintain stable economies at home and at the same time remain adequately prepared to meet the Communist threat of aggression not just this year or next year but for an indefinite period ahead.

COLLECTIVE SECURITY'S WEAK POINT [2]

Strategically, the problem [in the Far East] has developed along classical lines—the familiar case of a concentrated enemy in a central position deployed against scattered allies. Red China, inherently weak in industrial output for modern war but strong in manpower, engaged on three fronts—Korea, Indo-China and in civil war with Nationalist China. Fighting on all three simultaneously meant defeat, but individually the chances were excellent. The hope for victory depended on getting a cease-fire on some fronts so that the full potential of its limited military might could be thrown against the remaining one or ones.

That is what has happened and is happening. First was the cessation of the civil-war action by the isolation in the Formosa area which practically immobilized National China, one of the allies. Red China then concentrated against Korea and Indo-China. But even the double front was too much for its strained resources. So a cease-fire was obtained in Korea. This immobilized the so-called United Nations Forces and the South Koreans and left Red China free to concentrate on the third front—Indo-China and the French. Successful there, the Reds now turn back to the old first front located in Formosa. As Napoleon Bonaparte once said: "Give me allies as an enemy so that I can defeat them one by one."

[2] From an address by General Douglas MacArthur, former United States commander in the Far East, delivered before the American Legion in Los Angeles, January 26, 1955. *United States News & World Report.* 38:88. February 4, 1955. Reprinted from *United States News & World Report,* an independent weekly news magazine on national and international affairs published at Washington, D.C. Copyright 1955, United States News Publishing Corporation.

Militarily the situation demonstrates the inherent weakness of the theory of collective security—the chain is no stronger than its weakest link, and what is even more vital—its full power can only be utilized when all links are brought simultaneously into action. The diverse interests of allies always tend towards separation rather than unity. . . .

NEED FOR STRENGTH [3]

If we are to be true to our American heritage and our ancient foreign policy, our President must be supported now in strong policies, and the voices of courage and wisdom in our Congress must be strengthened. Had not the people, the press and the Congress spoken up clearly and firmly in the past, Formosa would have been surrendered as an appeasement to Red China, and even the Korean Republic might have been thrown in to seal the bargain. Such protests have blocked the attempt of the Chinese Reds to shoot their way into the United Nations.

Compromises are often necessary, but they should never be at the expense of our solemn pledges. They were urged even in the days of that great Roman, Marcus Aurelius. But his answer was: "Never esteem anything of value that would cause thee to break thy word, or lose thy self-respect." . . .

Now no one can pretend to read the minds of the Kremlin's inner circle. But we can see clearly their broad design of policy, which is to move quickly in on our weak spots, but always to avoid a major war. And, during the next two or three years, it is inconceivable that they will risk major war while they still lack that atom-bomb stockpile and those intercontinental bombers necessary to knock us out.

They have a healthy respect for our long-range air power, for our stockpile of fission bombs, for our sea power, which lets

[3] From "Catastrophe in Asia," article by General James A. Van Fleet, former commander of the United Nations forces in Korea. *United States News & World Report.* 37:26-8. September 17, 1954. Reprinted from *United States News & World Report,* an independent weekly news magazine on national and international affairs published at Washington, D.C. Copyright 1954, United States News Publishing Corporation.

us float air strips along key sectors of their perimeter, and for the industrial might back of all this.

Why should they, for the next few years, invite so terrible a retaliation—one in which they risk losing the home base for their world revolution? Their present policy—both skillful and prudent—of nibbling at our weak spots, has produced great gains for them, and fits their present situation.

But if we still have time, I don't say that time is on our side. Time is only and always on the side of those who know how to use it. And we have been solely preoccupied with preparing for that full-scale global war which may never come, and have been blind to the tepid wars which the Kremlin is winning, and which now threaten to outflank the free world. If this trend of the last eight years continues, we could lose World War III long before it begins.

To stop this disastrous nibbling away of our free world, we need an affirmative policy. A negative one, which contents itself only with checking the enemy now and then, but never stopping him or rolling him back, is not right for the genius of our people. Can Americans be expected to applaud a series of withdrawals, no matter how gallant, ending in a noble "disengagement"? To my thinking, this is only a prettier name for appeasement.

The affirmative policy we seek is one which will insure, in this world, the dominance of free societies, so that they may live in a free atmosphere where free men may freely exchange the product of free labor and of free ideas, moving toward wider horizons. Only in such a world can our American freedom survive.

Yet in this struggle for freedom, I feel I must sound one solemn warning. I believe in the United Nations. I applaud its successes in mediation, in relieving distress, and its efforts to improve world living standards. But it would be folly to rely on the United Nations as an instrument for collective security.

For instance, Russia and her European satellites are members of this "club." Other members are proudly "neutral" in our fight for freedom. Still others give only lip service to the cause. True, fifty of these United Nations joined us in the summer of

1950, denouncing aggression and calling for armed resistance—
in response to heavy American pressure. But when the chips
were down, only sixteen were willing to send forces to Korea
and, as Sir Winston Churchill has pointed out, America contributed 95 per cent of that total United Nations effort.

Just who really fought in Korea? The Republic of Korea
itself has at all times supplied all the divisions our policy makers
would let us arm and train—a limit of ten during the days of
hardest fighting, and sixteen at the date of the armistice.

America supplied seven divisions, plus those required in
Japan, and most of the naval and air support, as well as logistical
support for all, except for certain items for the Commonwealth
Division.

Now for the other United Nations. I have often expressed
my gratitude and high praise for the fighting qualities of the
men they sent. But here are the totals: a single division from
the entire British Commonwealth of Nations; a brigade from
Turkey; two batallions from Greece, and a battalion each from
Colombia, Ethiopia, the Philippines, Thailand, France, Holland
and Belgium.

The price we paid for them was the loss of decisive military
command. No important move could be made on the battlefield
without first securing, through Washington, the approval of a
caucus of sixteen diplomats halfway 'round the world. And,
after Red China entered the war, the enthusiasm of most of these
sixteen cooled rapidly. They controlled not only over-all strategy,
but small-scale tactical moves, and even the choice of bombing
targets within Korea.

For months during my stay there, the commander of the
magnificent Eighth Army was limited in his offensive moves to
actions requiring not more than a single platoon. And often I
feared the time might come when the caucus of diplomats might
take over from us command even of the platoons! To paraphrase
Sir Winston Churchill: Never in the history of combat has so
much authority been bought by so small a contribution!

Our superb fighting men plus the equally superb divisions of
the Korean Republic might have engaged and destroyed the
enemy. Instead they became pawns of that diplomatic caucus.

We had to appease our allies who feared offending Peiping. We had to appease "neutrals" who had piously joined in condemning aggression but who, when the call went out for fighting men, loftily sat on the fence. Above all, we appeased our enemies; if we offended them by fighting vigorously, they might not grant our plea for an armistice.

If we must again send our sons abroad to fight for freedom, I hope they go unshackled; that no appeaser's chains bind their arms behind their backs.

And I feel that the true road to collective security lies beyond the United Nations in regional pacts, like the Monroe Doctrine in the Americas, and others we have negotiated in the Pacific. In the frameworks of such smaller groupings, the nations involved can identify the aggressor, can appraise their rival interests, and can throw their whole united strength into their defense.

In such areas we can pick out brave allies anxious to defend themselves, and give them the aid they need.

Such pacts are tailor-made to fit the curious war which we, for eight years, have been losing to the Kremlin. If we can turn this tide, World War III may never come.

THE SOFT WAR [4]

What we face in Asia—and we face it now—is the possibility that new territories will fall to the enemy by a combination of subversion and guerrilla warfare. Such operations do not require masses of troops or modern equipment. They do not demand that Soviet or Chinese Communist troops cross borders and create, politically as well as militarily, targets for major American military strength. In Vietnam, Laos, Cambodia, Thailand, and possibly in Indonesia as well, the enemy is now conducting this targetless warfare in which he is a professional and we are amateurs.

[4] From *An American Policy in Asia* by Walt W. Rostow in collaboration with Richard W. Hatch, both associated with the Center for International Studies at Massachusetts Institute of Technology. Copublished by the Technology Press of MIT and John Wiley & Sons. New York. 1955. p42. Copyright 1955 by Massachusetts Institute of Technology. Reprinted by special permission.

Such aggression confronts the free world and the United States with a major challenge. It is clear that we cannot act alone to stem Vietminh activities in southern Vietnam. We can only be effective if the Vietnamese themselves and their government are prepared to resist; but, if they are prepared to resist, then the United States can contribute a significant margin of help. It should be recalled that communism has several times been set back by the free world in this kind of muted warfare: in the Philippines, where a few years back the situation was almost as precarious as in south Vietnam; in Burma, where on its own the newly independent government made an almost magical recovery from initial chaos; in Greece, where a substantial civil war had to be fought.

Success in resisting the combination of subversion and guerrilla operations depends directly on the political, economic, and social health of the area attacked. A substantial part of American and free world policy must be devoted to eliminating or preventing those circumstances under which subversion can succeed. . . . We live in a revolutionary world where rapidly changing societies may well be weak and vulnerable to the enemy's methods of aggression in certain phases of their history. It should be a major aim of American policy to prevent situations in Asia from degenerating to the point where guerrilla and other limited operations can take effective hold; but we must be prepared to meet them now and in the future.

Our military policy . . . must be a three-part policy: we must remain prepared to fight and win a total war; we must develop new capabilities for limited warfare, embracing the tactical use of atomic weapons; we must develop with our free world partners methods for dealing with subversive and guerrilla operations.

It is doubtful that we would reject the idea of a showdown with our enemies and adopt the more difficult and complex method for dealing with our enemies if we did not have faith that a successful frustration of Communist expansion by successfully building and maintaining economic and political health in the free world will eventually lead to changes within the Communist bloc that will diminish or end the present acute dangers under which we live. History affords few examples of peaceful transition of societies from totalitarianism (or acute autocracy) to more benevolent and peaceful forms of rule. Our modern experience with Hitler and Mussolini offers little hope. Bloody ware were required to end their rule. But a close examination of the changes now taking place in Soviet society and of the problems and dilemmas with which a successful free world would confront Communist China give limited grounds for maintaining faith in the possibility of a non-military resolution to the current struggle. We must keep our faith, but as we plan the peaceful courses of American political and economic action in Asia we must face the fact that they cannot succeed unless they are conducted within a framework of American and free world military capabilities covering the whole range from all-out atomic warfare to guerrilla and even lesser local subversive operations. And, within a general policy of minimizing the use of force, we must be prepared to use these capabilities when occasion demands.

THE SOCIAL CHALLENGE [5]

The revolution in Asia has two aspects. One is economic, the other is psychological and social. So far the Western powers have at least taken some note of the economic problem and have considered some marginal policies for dealing with it. But they have taken virtually no account at all of the psychological aspect. The Communists, on the other hand, have a program— crude, certainly, and evil—but nevertheless a program for dealing with both the economic and psychological upheaval in the world's backward areas. This fact gives them a head start over the West.

The starting point is the fact that there is only one road to the achievement of a dynamic economy—the road of capital accumulation and the building of industry. "Industrialization" is a magic word in the world's backward areas, a spell, a philosopher's stone of future prosperity. But the precondition

[5] From "The Challenge We Neglect in Asia," article by Barbara Ward, British writer and editor on foreign and economic affairs. New York *Times Magazine.* p13+. February 13, 1955. Reprinted by permission.

of industrializing an economy is to transform rural life, to do away with subsistence farming in closed village units, and to introduce an economy based upon the commercial exchange of goods.

This exchange enables the villages to become purchasers of manufactured goods—of what use is a local consumer industry which commands no market? It gives inducements to the farmer to increase his productivity and supply an urban population. And this margin of productivity is—short of foreign aid and investment—the chief source of saving and the means whereby laborers, now underemployed or merely idle in the village subsistence economy, are released to the towns and factories of the growing industrial sector.

Whether the process is carried on in the free enterprise economies of nineteenth-century Britain and America or under total dictatorship in twentieth-century Russia and China, the underlying shift is the same—the decay of the village, the rise of the town, the decline of static incomes derived from land, the growth of a vast wage and salary earning class. If Asia and Africa are ever to reach Western standards of health and consumption their road must be the same. There is no other.

But the village is far more than an economic unit. The village community is usually made up of families who, if not actually related, are all known to each other, and in more primitive tribal areas are actually part of the same kinship group. Collectively they farm their share of the village's communal land. They provide aid, security, backing and any necessary subsistence to any member of the group.

Village families in turn are ruled by a headman whose authority is almost parental as well as social, and they are guided by the priest, whose performance of ceremonies and rites marks the rhythm of the agricultural year, insures rain and fertility, provides the social order in the community and puts sanctions behind its social discipline.

Indeed, in more primitive communities; headman and priest are one. In short, the village is a complete society and one in which there is a high degree of those social attributes upon which the modern world tends to lay great stress—solidarity, interdependence, mutual aid, stability in the family unit, emotional security.

Just because village life is so all-inclusive, the impact upon it of an evolving industrial system is cataclysmic. The young Asian villager who goes away to the seaport or city tends to lose in one move the economic and emotional security of the family system and the social disciplines of local religion. Like the dazed rural workers of Britain in the 1830's, he finds himself in the featureless, friendless city, among a majority who, like him, seek feverishly for material advancement and change and who are uprooted from the traditional faith and sanctions of village life. The big cities of Asia—or Africa—today are fringed around with lawless shanty towns where the uprooted first-generation worker turns hooligan or fanatic under the pressure of bewilderment and despair. . . .

It is at this point that the effectiveness of Communist propaganda in such areas as Southeast Asia, India or tribal Africa begins to become apparent.

That Communist propaganda exploits the poorer peoples' desire for modernization hardly needs to be repeated. That Communist governments ruthlessly modernize their own peoples is common knowledge. But what is perhaps insufficiently considered is the extent to which, in the short run, the Communist approach meets the underlying social and psychological dilemmas of modernization.

The Communists not only uproot the villages, build the towns, recruit factory labor and reinvest ruthlessly the "savings" extracted from the under-consumption of the masses. In their crude, rough way, they also recreate the security of the village life. The omnicompetent state organizes social security, the party imposes group action and solidarity. Marxist-Leninism, the infallible "word" of the bureaucrats, produces the old concentration of spiritual and social power. . . .

This formidable appeal of communism to backward peoples —or indeed to comparably bewildered and uprooted groups in the wilderness of Western urban society—will hardly be withstood unless some comparable effort of policy and insight is achieved on the Western side. So far, our contacts are curiously haphazard. Our own commercial interest, together with a little foreign aid and a fraction of private investment, make up our quite inadequate contribution to massive modernization.

On the side of social evolution, Britain, foremost among the colonial powers, has worked to graft Western institutions on to primitive economies—but colonial authorities are necessarily suspect. The missionary churches make a great, though sometimes contradictory, contribution. Some private business firms have done pioneer work in the field of workers' housing and labor management. But of a major concerted Western effort to assist the backward areas over these perilous times of social readjustment, there is little trace.

There is, in fact, barely the realization that such an effort is necessary to counter the ceaseless confident pressure of Communist totalitarian faith. Materially and psychologically, the West is allowing the challenge of the backward areas to go largely by default.

Even with communism at the very door—as it is today in Southeast Asia—there is little disposition in the West to make long-term strategy for world development the first priority, not the last afterthought of Western diplomacy.

Yet the Communist inroad on Asia is already a fact and the risks in many parts of Africa are increasing. And behind this advance lies the possibility that when at last the stirrings and ambitions in Asia and Africa result in a world which is united in standards and technology as well as in aspiration, the stamp set upon it will be not the unforced unity of the free West, but the single collective strait-jacket of communism.

IDEAS, IDEALS AND NATIONALISM [6]

In the entire history of the American people it is doubtful that we have ever seen such a rapid sequence of military and political disasters as those we have faced in Asia during the last five years.

[6] From "Asians Fear Our Foreign Policy," article by Chester Bowles, former governor of Connecticut, advertising executive and United States ambassador to India. pb: The Pocket Book Magazine. 1:94-108. November 1954. Reprinted by permission.

In 1949, the Chinese Nationalist government collapsed before Mao Tse-tung's Red Army in spite of two billion dollars of American assistance.

In 1953, after three years of bitter warfare, a United Nations army, led by 450,000 Americans with the support of 600,000 South Koreans, accepted a status quo armistice at the thirty-eighth parallel in Korea. Because of this millions of Asians became convinced that American military power was not supreme, despite what they had assumed after our victory over Japan in World War II.

In Indo-China the Communist forces have defeated some of the finest troops of the French Union backed by another two billion dollars of American aid.

In Japan, where we offered our vanquished enemy a generous peace plus several billion dollars in economic assistance, we are facing political uncertainty and growing anti-Americanism.

India, the largest free nation in the world, is suspicious of our motives and fearful that the military support which we have given her neighbor, Pakistan, will eventually be used against her.

The situation calls for the most sober attention of the American people. Clearly we can no longer dismiss the people of India, Burma, Indonesia, Japan, and other Asian countries with such trite adjectives as "mysterious" and "inscrutable," nor can we buy security in Asia with tanks and machine guns alone. If we are going to build some bridge of understanding with the Asians before it is too late, we must come to grips with the political and economic forces which are shaping their ideas.

In order to develop such understanding we must talk less and listen more. Sometimes we will not like what we hear, and sometimes we will know beyond doubt that what we hear is unfair, untrue, distorted, or prejudiced. We must listen, nevertheless, and attempt to find answers that help bring us in tune with the restless, newly independent peoples who may eventually hold the balance of power in this divided world.

In my mind run hundreds of conversations I held with Asians of all types and social classes in many countries of the East. A talk I had with a keen and persevering science professor in Burma (who was as anti-Communist as he sounds unreasonably anti-American) forms the basis for the following dialogue. I hope it will suggest some of the bitter passions involved in the crucial relationship between the free West and free Asia.

Burmese Professor: It is tragic to see the mistakes you Americans have made in Asia. When World War II was over we expected so much of you. Now we are disillusioned and discouraged.

American Diplomat: You probably expected too much. After all, we are human beings like yourselves, with many limitations. We are not international meddlers by nature. We avoided World War II until 1941, when Pearl Harbor exploded us out of our isolationism. As soon as the war was over we disbanded our army only to find that the Soviet Union kept theirs and spent billions in its modernization.

Now we have responsibilities that no other nation in all history has even attempted to carry. We haven't sought the position that we hold, and we want no advantages of any kind. We are neither isolationists nor imperialists. All we are really striving for is peace and security and some means of stopping communism.

B.P.: I dislike communism just as much as you do. Indeed, my nephew was killed by Communist guerrillas in August 1951. Our government has been fighting the Communists for years and only recently has finally succeeded in defeating them. But you Americans have become so obsessed with your fears of communism that you are out of touch with the realities of Asia.

A.D.: How can we be too obsessed with it? You forget that the Communists are trying to overrun the world. Lenin laid down the Communist party objective over thirty years ago, and every Communist leader of importance since then has echoed it.

B.P.: That's true enough. But you Americans seem to feel that you can stop communism by dropping a bomb on it. Communism is not just an army or a place—it is an idea. It is a bad idea, to be sure, but even bad ideas cannot be killed by bombs. They can only be killed by better ideas.

We have always assumed that you Americans had a better idea. Most of us educated Asians have read your Declaration of

Independence; many of us know it by heart. Your Constitution has been a model for the democracies which we are attempting to create in Asia. . . .

What concerns us is that you Americans now seem to be turning your backs on your own long tradition of freedom and your belief in humanity. In your efforts to destroy communism in your own country you even seem ready to adopt the methods of communism.

A.D.: How can you say that we have departed from our democratic traditions? Look at our record in Asia following World War II. During the war many hundreds of thousands of young Americans were killed in an effort to free Asia from Japanese imperialism. President Roosevelt insisted that China be given a seat in the Security Council of the new United Nations as one of the five great powers. As soon as the war was over we gave the Philippines their freedom, just as we had said we would. We supported the freedom of India and Indonesia, and we gave the Japanese more help and encouragement than any other victor ever gave a former enemy.

B.P.: I know. But we cannot forget that you are part of the West which for generations took hundreds of millions of dollars of wealth each year from Asia to build up its cities, universities, and high standards of living and left us poor, illiterate, and close to the starvation line.

Even worse than the wealth the West took from Asia was the humiliation that we were made to feel. Because our skins were dark we were treated as second-class human beings. Only a few years ago our park benches had signs reading "For Europeans Only," and none of us were allowed to enter the British, Dutch, or French clubs except as servants. . . .

A.D.: But again I ask, why do you include America in this? We have never held any such colonial position in Asia. Fifty years ago we proposed the Open Door policy to keep China from being carved up by European powers, including Russia. In fact, we ourselves were the first nation to fight our way free from the colonial domination of Europe.

B.P.: Yes, but for all your professed friendship for pre-Communist China, you Americans kept your extraterritorial rights there until 1942, when the Japanese occupation made them worthless. And what have you been doing in the last few years? For one thing you have been propping up French colonialism in Indo-China. If you had taken a really strong position in 1946, the French would have pulled out as the British did in India, Pakistan, Burma, and Ceylon; and Vietnam, Cambodia, and Laos could have established their freedom. . . .

A.D.: We don't like European colonialism any better than you do, and we will agree that the French made many mistakes in Indo-China. But in Asia the colonialism that you are talking about is almost a thing of the past.

What you seem to ignore is the new Communist imperialism, supported by Moscow and Peiping, which is infinitely more dangerous. While you Asians are arguing about the outworn European colonialism, the new twentieth-century Communist colonialism will gobble you up.

B.P.: If you will let us alone, we Asians can defend our independence against communism a great deal better than you think. Just look at the record. In addition to the war in China there have been six civil wars in Asia since the end of World War II, all fostered and organized by Communists.

Four of them were in countries which had recently won their independence—the Philippines, Indonesia, Burma, and India—and in each of those four countries the Communists were crushed without any outside help. In the other two countries—Malaya and Indo-China—the Communists succeeded in creating major trouble. In Indo-China they have won a sweeping victory in spite of the combined military efforts of France and the United States.

Now why did the Communists fail in the four free countries of Asia, and why did they succeed in the two countries which were not free? Simply because in Indo-China and Malaya they were able to tell the people that they were leading an anti-imperialist war to drive the white colonial foreigners into the sea. In that way they were able to rally many millions of people who were not Communists. But wherever they have had to cope with Asian nationalism they have failed.

A.D.: Yes, but the Communists succeeded in winning in Indo-China only because the Chinese gave them arms.

B.P.: Why didn't the Chinese give the Burmese Communists arms? Because they knew that the Burmese Communists were opposing the will of the Burmese people, who had just won their freedom from the British and who were determined to defend that freedom. . . .

The trouble with you Americans is that you seem to see everything in terms of military power in spite of the clear fact that military power is not the controlling factor in much of the world. When the cream of the French army, backed by all your American equipment, failed to stop the Communists in Indo-China, you tried to prop them up with an alliance based on more alien white troops from Australia, New Zealand, and Britain supported by the two Asian countries which the rest of Asia believes are your satellites—Thailand and the Philippines. Although you kept telling us "if Indo-China falls to communism, all of Asia will fall," you scarcely bothered to discuss the problem with such Asian nations as India, which is immediately concerned and which carries weight and influence.

A.D.: Certainly India has great prestige, but she lacks military power.

B.P.: That reminds me of Stalin's cynical and stupid remark, "How many divisions has the Pope?" Power in Asia, I must repeat, is not a matter of divisions—it comes right down to *people*.

Why did the British leave India? Because they lacked military power? No. . . . But British military power could have held India for only a very few years against the united will of the people led by Gandhi. . . .

The Dutch tried to stop the tide of Indonesian nationalism with armed force. But they soon found that the will of eighty million people was too strong for all their tanks, equipment, and trained soldiers. Now in Indo-China the French have discovered the same ugly lesson at an infinitely greater cost.

When will you Americans learn that the problems of Asia are basically political and economic and that the military requirements are in a really subordinate position? . . . (. . . And so on, far into the night.)

This resentful and determined Asian offers arguments which represent the views of tens of millions of other Asians living between Calcutta and Tokyo.

He has no love for communism. He desperately wants to see democracy work. He wants to believe in America. He wants his own country to grow and develop toward new horizons of stability, prosperity, and peace. But he is troubled by the America which he sees today—an America that seems confused and out of touch with the people of the world who should be its friends. He is disturbed and also very much afraid.

His deep and often biased convictions carry an enormous weight in the scales of history which may counter-balance all of our weapons of war. We must listen to him, disagree with him when we think he is wrong, but listen.

American policies which continue to ignore the power of ideas that motivate turbulent modern Asia are policies doomed to catastrophic failure.

EXPANDING OUR INFORMATION PROGAM [7]

We must inject a greater vitality in our information and exchange programs, if we are to have any hope of counter-acting the depth of the barrage fired at us by Communist propaganda. It is high time we stopped regarding our information program as a kind of grudgingly tolerated stepchild, and back it up with adequate support.

I believe we have failed to understand just how effective a weapon this may be. We should greatly expand the program, particularly in Asia and the Middle East, where it is vital that it be administered by the most experienced talent available. For a job which is enormous we have been following a pattern of annual appropriations for our information program of about $80 million, which in comparison with our military program seems wholly inadequate.

[7] From address by Senator H. Alexander Smith (Republican, New Jersey), before the Senate March 22, 1955. Reprinted from a copy supplied by Senator Smith.

In our message to these areas, it is not enough that we take a negative approach against Soviet Russia. Stereotyped anti-Communist propaganda is, to some extent, wasted on people who may have been hearing for years that communism would release them from colonialism.

I would suggest, especially in the fields of motion pictures, libraries, and cultural-information officers, that our efforts should be greatly increased. In some respects a redirection of present expenditures, from Europe and Scandinavia to Asia, is called for. At present only about one third of the total funds being spent abroad by USIA [U.S. Information Agency] is being spent in the Near and Far East. This should be corrected.

There is no question that our exchange of persons program is becoming the most effective method for getting our message to the people of Asia. Undoubtedly it is sounder for Asians to convince Asians of our good motives and objectives than to leave that job to Americans. This can only be accomplished by bringing, for example, to our shores many more Indians, Burmese, Thais, Indo-Chinese, and others who are not familiar with our way of life. These young people thus may see at firsthand democracy in action, and have the opportunity to learn the technical and administrative skills so desperately needed in their own countries. Our experience with this program in the past has demonstrated conclusively how effective these people are in promoting mutual understanding and appreciation on their return to their homelands.

It is estimated in 1953 exchange visitors to the Soviet Union numbered about ten thousand persons. During that same year another ten thousand students from Southeast Asia visited Communist China. In contrast, of the 36,000 students, leaders, technicians, and teachers we are bringing to America under various public and private programs in fiscal 1955, only about four thousand are from Southeast Asia.

It is gratifying to see the favorable comparison in total figures, but disturbing to realize how far behind we are in terms of Southeast Asia.

The great majority of exchange visitors to America are under the auspices of private groups such as the foundations, and the labor and farmer organizations, whom I strongly commend for their outstanding work.

This entire exchange of persons operation, both public and private, which has been so successful, should be greatly expanded.

NATIONALISM AND INTERNATIONALISM [8]

Asian nationalism is a force that creates complex problems for the United States in any colonial land or even in a country in the still somewhat ambiguous position of Japan, but it should raise no great difficulties for us in the greater part of Asia, where the national regimes are fully and indisputably independent. On the contrary, we must look to nationalism as the chief force that can preserve the freedom of these Asian nations and thus help lay the foundations for a democratic world order of independent states. We must also look to nationalism to supply much of the ardor with which Asians must tackle their many serious economic, social, and political problems.

Under these circumstances, it is particularly discouraging to find nationalistic forces and American policy in apparent conflict with each other in many Asian countries. This unhappy situation can be attributed in part to the narrow prejudices and chauvinism that seem to accompany nationalism everywhere in the world, particularly in its nascent days. We see an undesirable side of nationalism in the basic suspicion of us as a Western nation which so complicates our relationship with Asian countries. Nationalism also provides its full share of discord between the individual lands of Asia, and this can all too easily embroil us too. For instance, . . . American military assistance to Pakistan stirs up such bitter resentment in India that we cannot but wonder if our aid in this case has not done more harm than good to the cause we wish to further.

American policy in Asia, however, has not run afoul of nationalism simply because of such specific problems. In the eyes

[8] From *Wanted: An Asian Policy,* by Edwin O. Reischauer, professor of Far Eastern Languages at Harvard University. Alfred A. Knopf. New York. 1955. p266-74. Reprinted by permission.

of many Asians a much more basic and serious conflict than this exists between American policy and their nationalistic aspirations. Every one of Asia's Communists, for example, has obviously become convinced that the United States represents a greater threat to the independence of his country than does the Soviet Union or the Communist system. What is even more disturbing, millions of non-Communist Asians seem to have come to the same conclusion. In fact, the majority of thinking Indians and Indonesians appear to be genuinely afraid of the United States, even if many of them may fear Russia more. This is, of course, a deplorable situation, and although in most countries it has not yet headed up into a specific crisis, it certainly creates fertile soil for the rapid growth of serious problems.

In the whole sphere of our foreign relations there has been no more tragic or inexcusable blunder than our failure to utilize or at least take necessary cognizance of the tides of nationalism in developing our Asian policies. . . .

A good case in point can be found in our attitude toward neutralism in Asia. . . . When we demand that Asian nations follow our lead and stand up and be counted on our side or declare themselves even more decisively on the field of battle, we are undoubtedly forcing our way against the emotional currents of Asia. Asians have for the most part only recently freed themselves from Western domination. Following the lead of any Western nation is scarcely appealing to them and may appear to be a dangerous reversion to the past. They like to cite, not without some smugness, George Washington's warning to the young American Republic to avoid foreign entanglements. The parallel is historically false, invalidated by the time differential of a century and a half that has put the contemporary Asian into an entirely different international situation from that which Washington knew. But the analogy is emotionally sound. No one can blame Asians for wishing to avoid involvement in international tensions that seem more remote to them than their own pressing internal problems of economic and political survival. In any case, Asians have no more desire to follow America's lead or, as they might put it, to fight America's battles than we had in our early years as a nation to follow Britain's lead or fight her wars.

But the real tragedy of our attitude toward Asian neutralism is our entire misunderstanding of what it really signifies in the war between democracy and communism. Asian neutralism is in reality a strong assertion of independence. It is so strong as to be ultimately unwise in the world in which we live, but basically it is the assertion of a point of view with which we sympathize wholeheartedly and on which we must place our greatest reliance for the future development of Asia. The democratic world order that we envisage depends upon this strong spirit of independence; communism in the long run can triumph only if this spirit is broken. The real strength of democracy is that anyone who is not specifically against it must ultimately be for it, while communism suffers from the great tactical liability that anyone who is not specifically for it is eventually forced to oppose it. Asian neutralism runs diametrically against Communist concepts of centralized, unified control, but for us it is just one of the many variations of the theme of independence that runs through all democracy. . . .

The importance of nationalism in the battle of Asia can hardly be overemphasized, but it would be a mistake for us to base our strategy entirely upon this one factor. Although the Communists have made skillful use of Asian nationalism, one of their chief appeals is their claim to represent a system of international government. Even in nationally aroused Asia, more and more people are looking beyond the ideal of national independence to a still higher ideal of world peace and order. Communism is not just an international conspiracy; it also purports to be a system of international peace. We may not be able to counter the very real dangers of the international conspiracy of the Communists until we have matched their international ideal. We also should not forget that our chief reason for desiring the development of truly independent nations throughout Asia is our hope that they will become healthy members of a democratic world order.

Each time we contribute to international cooperation through democratic means we are helping to build up the democratic answer to international communism. . . . The United States clearly cannot itself carry the whole burden of external assistance to Asians. In fact, much of the burden is already being borne by European nations. Not only have the French and British troops been fighting on the military battle line in Asia; the United Kingdom and the British Commonwealth nations are doing excellent work on the economic battle line through the Colombo Plan [See "Using the Colombo Plan" in Section III, above], and some other Western nations have at least small-scale economic endeavors under way. And on the ideological front we have perhaps been accomplishing proportionately less of value than have some of our Western allies.

Unfortunately we and our allies have often been working at cross-purposes. We sometimes say one thing in an Asian country and the British almost the opposite. The French have been fighting a valiant military battle in Indo-China, but on a political basis that has been defeating not only themselves but the whole democratic cause. There is perhaps a greater need for the coordination of Western democratic efforts in the battle of Asia than in the defense of Europe, just because the battle lines in Asia are less clearly defined and our weapons so much less certain in their use.

We should also realize that our Western allies can on the whole be more effective in Asia than can we. With the exception of the Philippines, it would be hard to find a country in Asia in which an individual Swede, New Zealander, or Belgian would not be in a better position to accomplish a job in either the economic or the ideological field than an American of comparable ability. The former would labor under fewer of the suspicions or resentments that are commonly directed toward Americans in Asia. In addition, higher American wage scales and greater opportunities for jobs here make it more difficult to obtain from the United States persons with high qualifications for work in Asia than it is from our Western allies.

An even more important reason for international cooperation in our Asian policies is that prevalent fears of American domination make Asians much more reluctant to accept aid from us than from an international agency. It is true that international agencies are often clumsy and slow-moving, but these drawbacks are more than offset by the simple fact that anything done through an international body in Asia, just because of its international cachet, has more chance of accomplishing its objectives than a comparable effort by the United States alone. Our general rule should be to approach each specific project through as large an international body as seems capable of handling it at all effectively, instead of emphasizing wherever possible the uniquely American character of our actions in Asia.

It would be even more advantageous if such international bodies also embraced all those in Asia who wished to take part. The greatest advantage of the Colombo Plan is that the participating Asian nations meet with the Western members as a council of equals. Such a fully international approach to the problem gives far more promise of ultimate success than a coordinated but exclusively Western approach. There are many technical skills to be exchanged between Asian nations, and any agency that could make the great surplus of technical abilities now lying dangerously dormant in Japan available for use throughout Asia would be doing both Japan and the rest of Asia a great service. Even more important than these considerations, the spirit of democratic equality of such a truly international system of Western aid to Asia would itself be an important part of the war of ideas and a significant step toward the development of an effective democratic system of world peace which can match in accomplishments the glittering but false claims of the Communists.

V. THE PROBLEM OF CHINA

EDITOR'S INTRODUCTION

This book has been mainly about United States policy toward free Asia. It has presented a survey of free Asian countries and a succession of different views on how American policy can strengthen these nations individually and collectively.

But a major factor in the Far Eastern situation today is, of course, United States policy toward Communist Asia and Communist Asia's policy toward us. Since the mainland of China fell to the Communists in 1949, many Asian events have been initiated by the Peiping regime. And Communist China has demonstrated uninterrupted hostility toward the United States, imprisoning American diplomats and civilians, intervening in the Korean war on the side of the Communist North Korean aggressors, sending aid that enabled the Communist-led Vietminh to win the crucial battle of Dienbienphu in Indo-China. After the negotiation of the truce for Indo-China, the Chinese Communists reaffirmed their intentions of taking Formosa and stepped up warfare against the islands off the Chinese mainland still held by the Nationalists. They also disclosed at the end of 1954 that 11 American air men captured during the Korean war had been sentenced to prison terms on charges of espionage. Release of the flyers was only brought about in August 1955 after considerable diplomatic pressure and bargaining; about forty imprisoned American civilians remained in Communist hands.

The United States has responded to these acts in various ways. Unlike Britain, India, and other nations, the United States did not extend diplomatic recognition to the Chinese Communist government when it established itself in Peiping, and the American delegation at the United Nations has consistently opposed Communist efforts—the Soviet Union has acted as spokesman for the demands—to have Red China take over the Chinese membership in the UN, including a permanent seat on the Security Council. When the Korean war broke out, President Truman ordered the United States Seventh Fleet to guard the Straits of Formosa, preventing both a Communist attack on the Nationalists and a Nationalist attack on the Communists. President Eisenhower, after taking office in 1953, announced that the fleet would not "continue to shield" the mainland from Nationalist attack. However, Washington has not encouraged such a Nationalist attack.

The possibility of war breaking out in the Formosa Straits arose in acute form in January 1955 when the Chinese Communists carried out a successful amphibious assault on Yikiang, an island near the Tachens, all held by the Nationalists. The United States fleet helped Nationalist troops evacuate the Tachens, a group 200 miles north of Formosa. What would the United States do, it was asked, if the Communists attacked Quemoy and the Matsus, islands close to the mainland shore and across the 125-mile wide straits from Formosa? By a treaty signed at the end of 1954, Washington was formally committed to defense of Formosa and the Pescadores (30 miles from Formosa). President Eisenhower refused to say whether or not American protection extended to the offshore islands as well, and the Senate passed a resolution which in effect left the decision in his hands.

American opinion has been united in some ways and divided in others on the many issues raised by these relations with Communist China. Few people want to see the Communists rewarded for their past aggression. Some, however, think that future recognition of Communist China should be considered if the Communists ever demonstrate they will accept peaceful international modes of conduct. Others believe the United States should help the Nationalists hold Quemoy and the Matsus; still others believe this will mean risk of a general war. The following articles present some of the arguments that have been current on the China problem.

A UN SEAT FOR RED CHINA? [1]

The issue of United Nations membership for Communist China and the related but separate issue of United States recognition have caused a good deal of trouble in the past six years. American politicians have treated the possibility of membership and recognition as virtually unmentionable. Some of our allies, having recognized the Communist regime in Peiping, have regarded the American position as irrational at best and possibly sinister; that is, they have wondered whether our non-recognition policy was the prelude to a military assult on the mainland in association with Chiang Kai-shek.

The lack of free world unity on Communist China and on the future status and role of Formosa has given Moscow and Peiping a handy issue which they have systematically exploited with vigor and with some success. They have portrayed the problem posed for the free world by Communist China as simply a matter of accepting an accomplished fact. They have used the issue of United Nations recognition in an attempt to split the United States from the rest of the free world; and they have succeeded in diverting attention and energy from the fundamental tasks of a free world policy in Asia. Many of our friends in the free world have been jockeyed into a position where they have come almost to believe that if only the United States would permit the entrance of Communist China into the United Nations all would be well in Asia. Many in the United States have come almost to believe that if only we could keep Communist China out of the United Nations we would be effectively frustrating Chinese Communist expansionist purposes.

From the point of view of Moscow, the absence of Peiping from the United Nations offers two advantages. It permits Moscow to pose as Peiping's international champion and to maintain a higher degree of Peiping's diplomatic dependence on Moscow than would otherwise exist. Thus, Moscow, while ostensibly the

[1] From *An American Policy in Asia* by Walt W. Rostow in collaboration with Richard W. Hatch, both associated with the Center for International Studies at Massachusetts Institute of Technology. Copublished by the Technology Press of MIT and John Wiley & Sons. New York. 1955. p53-4. Copyright 1955 by Massachusetts Institute of Technology. Reprinted by special permission.

ardent sponsor of United Nations membership for Peiping has in fact done little or nothing to alter the existing situation except to make proposals calculated to make Peiping's entrance into the United Nations more difficult.

We can assume that Peiping seeks a place in that international forum for two reasons: to enhance its prestige at home and in Asia and to diminish the degree of its diplomatic dependence upon Moscow. Peiping also desires the elimination of Formosa from the United Nations, an act that would strengthen its political hand at home and abroad and undermine the potential role of Formosa as a rallying point for the free Chinese.

From the perspective of our free world allies the failure to bring Communist China into the United Nations after they had recognized Peiping has been an inconsistency difficult to justify to their own people and in diplomatic debate. From the American perspective the United Nations issue has also been a difficult domestic and diplomatic issue that has posed sharply the question of our commitments to Formosa.

This brief outline of the principal issues involved in the membership problem underlines the fact that they are virtually all minor issues of political or psychological warfare in the narrow sense except the question of Formosa. Peiping's entrance into the United Nations if accompanied by Formosa's removal would have a disastrous effect on Formosa morale.

The pressure and emphasis given this issue by the Communist bloc and the free world's politicians have had, however, a distinctive result: if membership came now as the result of pressure, and despite United States opposition, Peiping could portray the event to the Chinese people and to the peoples of Asia as a Chinese Communist diplomatic victory and an American defeat.

When the military situation is stabilized, when the United States has set in motion on Formosa and in the rest of Asia positive policies designed to meet and ultimately to defeat the political and ideological challenge of Chinese communism, then we can deal with the recognition and membership issues from a position of strength. Under present conditions the voting of United Nations membership for Peiping would be an act of appeasement by the free world. It would be correctly taken by the peoples of Asia as a sign of the free world's weakness and lack of cohesion and purpose.

With Asia at peace, with a clear and positive free world policy launched, there would be a reasonable case for United Nations membership for Peiping: for United Nations membership does not imply approval, and it need not interfere with a constructive political role for Formosa. One essential purpose of the United Nations is that its membership be inclusive. It is a forum for the settlement of disputes short of war, and the one place where the free world and the Communist bloc confront each other in nonmilitary politics. These central functions limit the possible scope of United Nations action. But the existence and power of Communist China are unquestioned; and the presence of Communist China's representatives in the United Nations might assist in unifying the free world coalition, since that action would permit its members to take the measure of Peiping's policies and purposes without the confusion caused by the membership conflict.

At least three conditions should attach to Communist China's entrance into the United Nations quite aside from the return of our prisoners and the pacification of Korea, Indo-China, and the Formosa Strait. First, Communist China should not have a permanent seat on the Security Council. The permanent seat on the Security Council now held by Nationalist China should pass to an authentically independent Asian power, perhaps to India. Communist China has proclaimed itself a lean-to-one-side power, intimately tied to Moscow. It does not seriously pretend to status apart from its role in the Communist bloc. Even if that role is not one of pure subservience to Moscow, the Security Council seat should pass from Nationalist China to an independent Asian state. Second, Communist China's entrance into the United Nations should be accompanied by that of Japan and perhaps by the entrance of other states now outside the world organization. The review of the United Nations Charter in the course of 1955 [and thereafter] may be the proper occasion to recognize that the weaknesses of the United Nations caused by the split among the world's powers should be compensated for at least partially by more nearly total world participation. Third, Formosa should retain a seat in the United Nations Assembly.

Whether or not Peiping would accept such terms for entrance into the United Nations, it may be well for the free world to agree on some such terms and make them known. For the United Nations recognition issue has been costly to the United States, not because Peiping's presence in New York would be helpful, but because this issue has divided the free world and inhibited other more important lines of common action in Asia.

AN OFFICIAL VIEW [2]

I am often asked why the United States Government is firmly opposed to recognition of the Chinese Communists and giving them a seat in the United Nations. We are confronted in Peiping with an arrogant, contemptuous regime of hardcore international Communists who have played a gangster role in their relations with us and other countries, the latest example being their sentencing, as spies, United Nations prisoners of war held in flagrant violation of the Korean Armistice. [The prisoners were released in August 1955 after thirty-two months of imprisonment.—Ed.]

They have thrown our citizens into jail without trial, they have tortured and brain-washed our prisoners of war, they have blackmailed our businessmen, they have confiscated our properties. They respect no law divine, international or domestic, unless it suits their purposes to do so. They speak not for the great Chinese people and nation but for international communism.

These defiant imposters in Peiping come no closer to representing the true interests and aspirations of their country than do William Z. Foster and his cohorts in this country, or Palmiro Togliatti in Italy, or Maurice Thorez in France. They are all part and parcel of the apparatus of the international Communist

[2] From "The Growing Partnership Among Free Nations," address by Walter S. Robertson, Assistant Secretary of State for Far Eastern affairs, delivered before the Chamber of Commerce of Greater Philadelphia, January 13, 1955. *United States Department of State Bulletin.* 32:130-1. January 24, 1955.

conspiracy. Their objectives are the antithesis of the principles which constitute the foundation of the United Nations Charter. They are dedicated to the destruction of everything the United Nations stands for.

The regime stands convicted by the United Nations of the crime of aggression. It has not expiated that crime, nor its crimes against countless innocent victims of Communist malevolence. Its admission to the United Nations would undermine the real Chinese Government, now based on Formosa, which is the one remaining hope of millions of Chinese on the mainland and scattered about the world who despise communism and refuse to accept as permanent the Communist enslavement of their country.

Our Government is opposed to any action which would strengthen the international prestige of Chinese communism, or its capability for advancing its design for further conquests in collusion with Soviet communism. We should do nothing which would betray the hopes of the Chinese with the will to resist Communist domination. Our recognition of Communist China and acquiescence in giving this contemptuous aggressor against the peace of the world a seat in an organization dedicated to maintaining the peace of the world would in our considered view have calamitous effects upon the United Nations itself and on the cause of freedom everywhere. . . .

The concept that the economic difficulties of free nations in Asia can be substantially alleviated by expanding trade with Communist China is, in my opinion, erroneous. The economy of mainland China is rigidly controlled by the Chinese Communist regime, and the foreign trade of Communist China is systematically regulated by the regime in terms of its political objectives and its five-year economic-development plan. No export or import trade is licensed which, in the estimation of the Communist masters of mainland China, would not serve their aggressive purposes, directly or indirectly.

The Chinese Communist interest in trade expansion is limited principally to items of industrial and military importance. The regime is committed to a program of industrial expansion designed to increase its war-making potential. It must import from the free world in order to realize its goals. In order to pay for its imports it must export.

The measure of the ruthlessness with which the Chinese Communists pursue their program is seen in the fact that exports of foodstuffs from mainland China have continued undiminished despite the catastrophic flood of last summer, which inundated an estimated 10 per cent of the farm land of mainland China. The specter of starvation of additional thousands of flood victims did not for one moment deter the Communists from the exportation of food in exchange for essential items of war supplies, industrial machinery and strategic materials such as rubber.

The Communists employ food as a weapon of war. It matters not how many of its 600 millions starve. Even the Communist Army has had to be put on food rations. To carry out its objectives, the regime must build up its economic structure and war machine. The importation of "non-essential" consumer goods has no place in the Chinese Communist scheme of things. No benefit not fraught with the greatest danger could be derived by the free-world countries from a large expansion of their trade with Communist China.

No, unrestricted trade with Communist China is not the answer. The answer lies in closer cooperation among the free countries from a platform of mutual security. Such a platform was constructed at Manila and it is small wonder that while it was being built the Chinese Communists resorted to every device of propaganda to intimidate and divide the free nations who would oppose them.

U. S. POLICY AND FORMOSA [3]

The United States is firmly committed to the defense of Formosa and the Pescadores. These islands became part of the Japanese Empire in 1895. They continued as such for half a

[3] From "Our Foreign Policies in Asia," address by Secretary of State John Foster Dulles delivered before the Foreign Policy Association, New York, February 16, 1955. *United States Department of State Bulletin.* 32:329-30. February 28, 1955.

century, until they were relinquished by Japan as a result of her defeat in war—a defeat principally wrought by the efforts and sacrifices of the United States.

These islands form an important part of the Western Pacific defense system. . . . The people of the islands eagerly seek our help.

Thus Formosa and the Pescadores have been properly a matter of concern to the United States.

In 1945 our long-time ally, the Republic of China, was entrusted with authority over these islands. In 1950, when the aggression against Korea occurred, President Truman ordered our Pacific Fleet to defend Formosa against possible Chinese Communist attack. Now that determination has been converted into our Mutual Defense Treaty with the Republic of China.

It is important to note that the treaty, except as it relates to United States territories, covers only the islands of Formosa and the Pescadores, and an armed attack directed against those islands. The congressional authority is to secure and protect Formosa and the Pescadores against armed attack, and to make secure and to protect "related positions and territories" as the President judges this would be "required or appropriate in assuring the defense of Formosa and the Pescadores."

The President did not use our armed forces to help the Chinese Nationalists to hold the Tachen islands and Yushan and Pishan, lying some 200 miles north of Formosa. These islands were virtually unrelated to the defense of Formosa and the Pescadores. We helped the Chinese Nationalists to evacuate these islands and regroup their forces, so as to avoid a bloody and wasteful battle which would have inflamed public emotions. Thus, Nationalist China and the United States have made an important contribution to the cause of peace.

It has been suggested that Nationalist China should go further and surrender to the Chinese Communists the coastal positions which the Communists need to stage their announced attack on Formosa. It is doubtful that this would serve either the cause of peace or the cause of freedom.

The Chinese Communists have been the initiators of violence in this area. They have already formally declared their intention to take Formosa by force. If the Chinese Nationalists now oblige by making it easier for the Chinese Communists to conquer Formosa, will they be less apt to do so? I doubt it.

The United States has no commitment and no purpose to defend the coastal positions as such. The basic purpose is to assure that Formosa and the Pescadores will not be forcibly taken over by the Chinese Communists. However, Foreign Minister Chou says they will use all their force to take Formosa and they treat the coastal islands as means to that end. When the Nationalists voluntarily evacuated the Tachen islands, the Chinese Communists' comment was: "the liberation of these islands has created favorable conditons for our People's Liberation Army in the liberation of Formosa."

Thus the Chinese Communists have linked the coastal positions to the defense of Formosa. That is the fact which, as President Eisenhower said in his message to Congress about Formosa, "compels us to take into account closely related localities." Accordingly, we shall be alert to subsequent Chinese Communist actions, rejecting for ourselves any initiative of warlike deeds.

It is hardly to be expected that the Chinese Communists will renounce their ambitions. However, might they not renounce their efforts to realize their goals by force?

Such renunciation of force is one of the basic principles of the United Nations, and the United States had hoped, and still hopes, that the United Nations may be able to effect a cessation of the present hostilities. President Eisenhower, in his message to Congress dealing with this matter, made clear that the United States would welcome action by the United Nations which might bring an end to the active hostilities in the area. . . .

A great danger in Asia is the fear of many non-Communist peoples that the United States has no real intention of standing firmly behind them. Already that fear has mounted to the danger point. We accepted in Korea an armistice which the Chinese Communists boisterously misrepresent as a "victory" for them. We acquiesced in an Indo-China armistice which reflected the defeat of the French Union forces at Dienbienphu. We aided the Tachen evacuation. The reasons were compelling; nevertheless the result added a few square miles to the Communist domain.

If the non-Communist Asians ever come to feel that their Western allies are disposed to retreat whenever communism threatens the peace, then the entire area could quickly become indefensible.

As the situation now exists, neither the cause of freedom, nor United States security, nor world peace and security would be promoted by undermining the faith of the free Asian peoples in our strength and in our willingness to use that strength to restrain those who violently menace liberty. The American people have, through the Congress, made their own resolution clear. That is a verdict which the Government accepts as sound and which it will soberly execute.

FORMOSA, QUEMOY, AND THE MATSUS [4]

How . . . shall we mend the walls of our coalition? And how shall we frustrate the supreme aim of the Moscow-Peiping Axis, which is to drive a wedge between America and her allies? And is there any hope of a peaceful solution of the offshore island question?

I think so, and . . . so I would urge our Government to promptly consult our friends, yes, and the uncommitted states, too, and ask them all to join with us in an open declaration condemning the use of force in the Formosa Strait, and agreeing to stand with us in the defense of Formosa against any aggression, pending some final settlement of its status—by independence, neutralization, trusteeship, plebiscite, or whatever is wisest.

Nor do I see any reason why we should not invite Soviet Russia, which is united by treaty with Red China, to declare its position, to indicate whether it prefers the possibility of ultimate settlement by agreement to an unpredictable, perhaps limitless,

[4] From address by Adlai E. Stevenson, 1952 Democratic Presidential nominee, delivered by radio, April 11, 1955. Text from New York *Times.* p4. April 12, 1955.

conflict, started by an arrogant, foolhardy Communist China either by design or by miscalculation.

Fortified by such an international declaration denouncing the use of force, with the assurance of such collective support for the defense of Formosa, and with the addition thereby of moral solidarity to military strength, I should think that Quemoy and Matsu would have little further importance to the Nationalists, let alone to us. And that they could then be relinquished before we stumble any further down the dismal road to war that nobody wants.

Diplomacy prescribes no rigid formula for accomplishing our objectives, and another major avenue in the quest for a peaceful solution in the Far East remains unexplored: the United Nations. I should think that the United States, together with friends and allies in Europe and Asia, could submit a resolution to the United Nations General Assembly, calling upon the Assembly likewise to condemn any effort to alter the present status of Formosa by force. And I think we could afford to go further and call upon the United Nations Assembly to seek a formula for the permanent future of Formosa, consistent with the wishes of its people, with international law, and with world security.

One of the weaknesses of our position is that we have been making Formosa policy as we thought best regardless of others.

We have not made it clear that we are helping to hold Formosa, not as an offensive but as a purely defensive measure. We have not made it clear because the Administration has not been clear itself. But we can't expect other nations to support policies they disagree with, let alone ambiguous and dangerous policies.

Joint action along the lines I've indicated would put Formosa policy on a much broader and a more comprehensive basis. In the eyes of the Asian nations, we would thereby achieve a consistent and morally unquestionable position in providing for the protection of the Formosans according to the principles and the ideals of international law.

In the eyes of our European friends and allies we would once more have asserted our full belief in the value, indeed in the indispensability, of maintaining the alliance of the free world against the slave world. And in the eyes of our Nationalist friends on Formosa, surely the understanding and the support of the bulk of the non-Communist world is a much stronger defense of Formosa than these islands can possibly be.

But if the Chinese Communists refuse; if they insist on force and reject any peaceful solution, then at least it would be clear to everyone who the aggressors were. And, clearly, if the Chinese are so bent on violence, so intoxicated by their success, so indifferent to the grisly realities of modern war, then we have no alternative but to meet force with force. But let us at least meet it with our allies beside us and the blame placed squarely where it belongs—not on America's fantasies and inflexibility, but on the unteachable and unquenchable ambition and the indifference to human life of China's Communist regime.

DRAWING THE LINE [5]

I was amazed and shocked by the speech of Adlai Stevenson on . . . [April 11, 1955, reprinted above]. He not only appears to be giving the green light to the loss of Quemoy and Matsu, but he also cast reflection upon the future of the island of Formosa itself.

Less than two months after the Congress approved the Formosa resolution by a vote of 409 to 3 in the House and 85 to 3 in the Senate and after the ratification of our mutual defense pact with the Republic of China by a vote of 64 to 6, Mr. Stevenson stated that we should seek to get certain of our allies to line up with us in the defense of Formosa against any aggression "pending some final settlement of its status—by independence, neutralization, trusteeship, plebiscite, or whatever is wisest."

What a way to build confidence in our ally, with whom we have just entered into a mutual defense treaty.

There was no suggestion by Mr. Stevenson that there might be a plebiscite on the mainland of China to see if the Chinese

[5] From address by Senator William F. Knowland (Republican, California), Republican leader in the Senate, before the Indiana Republican Editorial Association, Indianapolis, April 16, 1955. Reprinted from text supplied by Senator Knowland.

are satisfied with their loss of freedom by Communist aggression supported by the Soviet Union.

Does not Mr. Stevenson know that the free people of China would look upon a United Nations trusteeship as only a form of multiple colonialism for such a trusteeship would undermine if not destroy the sovereignty of the Republic of China?

Certainly the Republic of China will not consent to a United Nations or any other type of trusteeship over the island of Formosa. . . .

What sense does it make to on the one hand be building a collective security system in the Far Pacific and on the other giving consideration to the neutralization of one third of the available non-Communist armed forces in that area of the world. During the early days of our Republic we had an expression "United we stand, divided we fall."

As a matter of national policy are we now to preach a doctrine for our friends abroad "Divided you stand until the Communists gain sufficient strength to make you fall?"

As one American, I get no satisfaction at all from a divided Korea, a divided Germany, or a divided Vietnam. I see nothing in either example that should want us to put our stamp of approval on a divided China which is the meaning of a so-called two Chinas policy.

Let's put ourselves in the unlikely position of facing the situation wherein Communist forces, by armed action supported by the Soviet Union, should be able to take over mainland America and our Government was temporarily forced to the Territory of Hawaii or Alaska. Would we accept a two-Americas policy? Would we give up the effort to restore constitutional government to our people and to our homeland? The answer is, of course, a resounding "No" on both counts.

There will never be an easy solution to the problems facing this country and the free world. Whenever a line is drawn there will be cogent reasons advanced for making it at some other time or place.

There are some who oppose the drawing of the line at Quemoy and Matsu who say that they would be willing to stand on the line of Formosa and the Pescadores, but would they really be willing to stand even there?

Will they not, like some of the British, Prime Minister Nehru, and Adlai Stevenson, then begin to throw doubt even upon the future of Formosa?

In a final desperate effort to avoid facing up to the realistic issue of Communist aggression, will they at that point urge that the problem be thrown into the United Nations?

There a combination of the Communist nations, neutralist powers, and some of our fair-weather friends presently tending toward a "peace at any price policy" could join forces in agreeing to a Far Eastern Munich that will give to the Communists at a conference another substantial victory at the expense of the Republic of China.

The smaller nations of the world should stop, look, and listen before they join their voices to those of the other appeasers. If the Republic of China, with 9.5 million people, can be sold down the river at a Far Eastern Munich so then could the more than thirty independent nations having populations of less than that figure.

With the record of a quarter century of broken agreements by the Soviet Union, I have questioned the advisability of entering into another meeting of the heads of state until the Soviet Union has shown by deeds rather than words that they are prepared to respect agreements entered into.

Yalta should have been a warning signal to the American people that there is no moral right for large nations, including our own, to distribute the territory and the people of our allies such as was done with Poland and with China.

The rather dubious argument is advanced that the Soviet forces were already in occupation of Poland and would have been in a position to occupy much of China if we had not consented to their demands.

Since when has America come to subscribe to the strange new doctrine that if the bandit is in possession of the loot he should be given a clean bill of health morally and a legal title to the same?

Have we allowed international morals to fall so low that we now are prepared to accept the doctrine that might makes right?

I think not. Any public officials who in the future, regardless of the party in power, try to shackle the moral position of the American people in such chains will, in my judgment, be overwhelmingly repudiated.

LEADERSHIP AGAINST COMMUNISM [6]

In general Communist China constitutes a challenge to all the non-Communist world, and here lies the real significance of the first five years of Mao's regime.

There is first of all a challenge to face up to the threat posed, not to take our eyes off the fundamental structure and doctrine of this Communist state when its leaders attempt to distract our attention with gaudy banners and displays proclaiming peace. It is vital to remember that the goals and the conflicts remain unchanged. Communist China will, whenever expedient, continue to promote revolution, violence, and intrigue abroad and to apply in surrounding areas the strategy which has brought success thus far.

It has become clear in these last years that Western policy must oppose the further spread of communism. This is a task to tax the wisest minds. It involves creating unity and determination among sovereign states with free institutions, some of which are in disagreement as to the nature of the threat. It necessitates coping with totalitarian techniques of propaganda and hidden aggression against which few defenses have so far been markedly effective. It calls for analysis, understanding, sacrifice, and hard work. Such efforts are unlikely to be made unless the threat is understood and the struggle seen to be what the Communists say it is: implacable.

There is need for dedication to the cause of breaking the power of this tyranny. But up to now we have seemed able to

[6] From *China Under Communism, The First Five Years*, by Richard L. Walker, assistant professor of history at Yale University. Yale University Press. New Haven, Conn. 1955. p326-8.

think in terms of only one method: war. This possibility is naturally in the minds of many Chinese, both in and outside Communist China. After one year of the Mao regime a British missionary reported: "The Chinese can see no hope for the future—no hope except the third world war. While the rest of the world talks of it with fear and anxiety, the Chinese eagerly await it. . . ." But the costs of war today make this an almost impossible choice. There is therefore heavy obligation placed upon statesmen, scholars, and thoughtful citizens to comprehend the nature of the new Communist despotism and to discover if possible those weaknesses which can make its power disintegrate internally, as the Communists expect institutions outside their areas of control to disintegrate.

As the greatest power outside the Iron Curtain, the United States is perforce a leader against the Communist forces pledged to its destruction. Our position, as we are becoming increasingly aware, requires a fine balance between restraint and patience on the one hand and firmness and determination on the other. We are challenged to match our power with our statesmanship. But perhaps in the long run the challenge goes even deeper. It reaches into the whole philosophy and educational system of America today. Leadership involves training civil servants and a people equipped to understand their obligations. Our global role demands that we no longer instruct our children about our Western civilization alone and send out into the world representatives and travelers with a haughty Western ethnocentrism which has already cost us much respect in many areas of the world. We will fail in our role of bringing about a coalition of free nations unless we can educate our people to be capable of appreciating other cultures and approaching them with a degree of humility. If our faith is to be in humanity as opposed to despotism, it is imperative for us to understand that neither the West nor the United States has a monopoly of human values or achievements.

In the non-Communist areas of Asia as well as other economically underdeveloped areas of the world the United States has the opportunity to aid in creating alternatives which the people will choose instead of communism. This will require imaginative action as well as cooperation with our allies in the resolve to eliminate colonialism. It may involve, for example, a cooperative plan for economic development dwarfing even the Marshall Plan. It may mean guaranteeing against aggression both the results of economic assistance and the security of the people involved. However great the cost of such creative responses to the Communist challenge it will be insignificant compared to the cost of failure to take up the challenge.

Communist China's threat to the United States also means, I believe, that we must maintain the strength to oppose it. But a determination not to allow this new Communist colossus to score further victories demands vigilance as well as strength. The Communist leaders must not be allowed to win tactical victories of propaganda or to split us from our allies. I believe that such vigilance involves also a continued refusal to recognize Communist China. Recognition cannot but be interpreted as acquiescence in the subjection of a great people and a rich culture to oppression. And in the global battle which according to Mao Tse-tung is so all embracing that " 'neutrality' is only a term for deceiving people" it is vital that the Chinese people retain in Taiwan [Formosa] a symbol which will keep alive the hopes of those within the Iron Curtain and serve as a rallying point for those outside it.

The Communist despotism which has been erected in their land constitutes a grave challenge for all those Chinese who remain free, and especially for the government on Taiwan. There is an injunction placed upon the leadership and people there to learn from their past, to reassess the values and the meaning of their traditional civilization in today's complicated world, and to help make this symbol one to which free Chinese can with hope pledge their faith and future. The way in which the world outside the Iron Curtain reacts to the challenge of Communist China may well determine whether the recrudescence of oriental despotism in an even more oppressive form is a passing moment in China's long history or the fate of the whole world.

BIBLIOGRAPHY

An asterisk (*) preceding a reference indicates that the article or a part of it has been reprinted in this book.

BOOKS, PAMPHLETS, AND DOCUMENTS

*Battistini, L. H. Japan and America. 198p. John Day Co. New York. '54.

Bowles, Chester. Ambassador's report. 415p. Harper & Bros. New York. '54.

*Castle, E. W. Billions, blunders and baloney. 278p. Devin-Adair Co. New York. '55.

*Dangerfield, Royden. New Japan. (Headline Series no 102) 62p. Foreign Policy Association. New York. '53.

Durdin, Tillman, and Smith, R. A. China and the world. (Headline Series no99) 63p. Foreign Policy Association. New York. '53.

Griswold, A. W. Far Eastern policy of the United States. 530p. Harcourt, Brace & Co. New York. '38.

Hammer, E. J. Struggle for Indo-China. 342p. Stanford University Press. Stanford, Cal. '54.

Hanson, Haldore, and others. Partnership for freedom: proposals for world economic growth. 52p. Union for Democratic Action Educational Fund. Washington, D.C. '55.
   Available from Americans for Democratic Action. 1341 Connecticut Ave. Washington 6, D.C.

*Henderson, William. New nations of southeast Asia. (Headline Series no 110) 62p. Foreign Policy Association. New York. '55.

Javits, J. K. Progressive and dynamic force in government; address delivered before the Alumni Federation of Columbia University, New York, December 29, 1954. 5p. mimeo. The Author. 630 Fifth Avenue. New York 20. '54.

Kennan, G. F. Realities of American foreign policy. 120p. Princeton University Press. Princeton, N.J. '54.

*Knowland, W. F. Address before Indiana Republican Editorial Association, Indianapolis, April 16, 1955. Text supplied by Sen. Knowland.

Latourette, K. S. History of modern China. 234p. Penguin Books. London. '54.

Michener, J. E. Voice of Asia. 331p. Random House & Bantam Books. New York. '51.

Pratt, J. W. History of United States foreign policy. 808p. Prentice-Hall. New York. '55.
   Struggle for eastern Asia. p730-53.

Purcell, Victor. Malaya: Communist or free? 288p. Stanford University Press. Stanford, Cal. '54.

Quan, Lau-king. Introduction to Asia, a selective guide to background reading. 214p. Library of Congress. Reference Department. Supt. of Docs. Washington 25, D.C. '55.

*Reischauer, E. O. Wanted: an Asian policy. 276p. Alfred A. Knopf. New York. '55.

Robequain, Charles. Malaya, Indonesia, Borneo, and the Philippines; tr. by E. D. Laborde. 456p. Longmans, Green & Co. London. '54.

Romulo, C. P. Crusade in Asia. 309p. John Day Co. New York. '55.
    Same abridged. United States News & World Report. 38: 82-90+. Ap. 15, '55.

Roosevelt, Eleanor. India and the awakening East. 237p. Harper & Bros. New York. '53.

*Rostow, W. W., and Hatch, R. W. American policy in Asia. 59p. Technology Press of Massachusetts Institute of Technology and John Wiley & Sons. New York. '55.

Schwantes, R. S. Japanese and Americans. 380p. Harper & Bros. for Council on Foreign Relations. New York. '55.

*Smith, H. A. Address before the Senate, March 22, 1955. 15p. Printed text supplied by Senator Smith.

*Stassen, H. E. Address at the tenth anniversary banquet of the AMVETS, December 10, 1955. 10p. mimeo. Foreign Operations Administration. Washington, D.C. '55.

Trager, F. N., and Trager, H. G. Burma: Land of golden pagodas. (Headline Series no 104) 64p. Foreign Policy Association. New York. '54.

*Trumbull, Robert. India since independence. (Headline Series no 105) 62p. Foreign Policy Association. New York. '54.

United States. Foreign Operations Administration. American universities in technical cooperation. 15p. Foreign Operations Administration. Washington, D.C. [1954]

*United States. Foreign Operations Administration. Mutual Security Program, fiscal year 1956, a summary statement. 87p. Foreign Operations Administration. Washington, D.C. May 1955.

United States. Foreign Operations Administration. Technical cooperation in agriculture. 16p. Office of Public Reports. Foreign Operations Administration. Washington, D.C. n.d.

United States. Foreign Operations Administration. Technical cooperation programs around the world. 18p. Office of Public Reports. Foreign Operations Administration. Washington, D.C. [1954]

*United States. Foreign Operations Administration. Thailand. (Country Series) Foreign Operations Administration. Washington, D.C. n.d. Leaflet.

United States. Mutual Security Agency. Mutual security in southeast Asia. Mutual Security Agency. Washington 25, D.C. n.d. Leaflet.

*United States. Senate. Committee on Foreign Relations. Mutual security act of 1955; hearings, May 5-23, 1955, before the committee on the mutual security program for fiscal year 1956. 556p. 84th Congress, 1st session. Supt. of Docs. Washington 25, D.C. '55.
  Reprinted in this book: Statement by Admiral Arthur Radford. p97-100.

*Walker, R. L. China under communism: the first five years. 403p. Yale University Press. New Haven, Conn. '55.

PERIODICALS

Atlantic Monthly. 194:4-7. Jl. '54. Pakistan.

Atlantic Monthly. 195:16-19. Ja. '55. Rural India.

Atlantic Monthly. 195:4-8. F. '55. Indonesia.

Christian Century. 72:704-5. Je. 15, '55. Singapore after the riots. H. A. Jack.

Christian Science Monitor. p9. Je. 10, '55. Time is running out on south Vietnam. Gordon Walker.

Christian Science Monitor. p15. Je. 14, '55. India's diplomat without portfolio. Neal Stanford.

Collier's. 135:46-7+. Ap. 1, '55. Who can save Asia? Delia and Ferdinand Kuhn.

Collier's. 135.66-9. My. 27, '55. 'Way down upon the Irrawaddy. Delia and Ferdinand Kuhn.

Commentary. 19:415-20. My. '55. Mr. Eisenhower's Far East policy. Harold Lavine.

Congressional Record—Senate. 101:(daily) 4226-8. Ap. 25, '55. Foreign policy address. W. F. George.

Foreign Affairs. 33:54-71. O. '54. Fresh look at free Asia. Chester Bowles.

Foreign Affairs. 33:72-85. O. '54. Spotlight on Thailand. E. F. Stanton.

Foreign Affairs. 33:86-97. O. '54. Ho Chi Minh: disciplined Communist. Ruth Fischer.

Foreign Affairs. 33:360-75. Ap. '55. United States foreign policy and Formosa. Arthur Dean.

Foreign Affairs. 33:535-47. Jl. '55. Bad and good in us. P. H. Douglas.

Foreign Affairs. 33:548-65. Jl. '55. Mind of Asia. M. R. Masani.

Foreign Policy Bulletin. 33:1-2. F. 15, '54. Honest elections in Philippines. J. J. Dalton.

*Foreign Policy Bulletin. 33:5-7. Ag. 1, '54. Burma and Malaya: jungle war against communism. S. K. Padover.

Foreign Policy Bulletin. 33:1-2. S. 1, '54. What next in Thailand. R. J. Coughlin.

Foreign Policy Bulletin. 34:68-9. Ja. 15, '55. Should U.S. recognize Peiping? Nicholas Roosevelt.

Foreign Policy Bulletin. 34:83. F. 15, '55. Has U.S. China policy changed? Neal Stanford.

Foreign Policy Bulletin. 34:84-5. F. 15, '55. Should U.S. recognize Peiping? W. F. Knowland.

Foreign Policy Bulletin. 34:86-8. F. 15, '55. India: an Asian success story. V. M. Dean.

*Foreign Policy Bulletin. 34:117. Ap. 15, '55. Should U.S. aid other countries? G. W. Malone.

Foreign Policy Bulletin. 34:132-4. My. 15, '55. Five views on Formosa. J. F. Dulles, A. E. Stevenson, Chester Bowles, T. K. Finletter, W. F. Knowland.

Life. 38:29-37. My. 2, '55. Friends of the West speak up.

Life. 38:138-54. My. 2, '55. How a citadel for freedom was destroyed by the reds. Lin Yutang.

*Harper's Magazine. 208:78-84. Je. '54. An unsentimental look at India. H. D. Gideonse.

Harper's Magazine. 209:36-43. Ag. '54. Indonesia: the fabulous experiment. Cameron Hawley.

*Newsweek. 45:48. Ap. 18, '55. Asian friend of ours. E. K. Lindley.

*Newsweek. 45:38. Ap. 25, '55 Nehru and us: some advice. E. K. Lindley.

Newsweek. 65:32-4. My. 2, '55. Chou's tricky performance at Bandung.

*Newsweek. 45:39. My. 23, '55. Threats to Thailand. E. K. Lindley.

*New York Times. p E5. Ap. 11, '54. A.B.C.'s of Indo-China.

New York Times. p E1. Jl 25, '54. News of the week in review, the war.

New York Times. p E8. N. 28, '54. "Toil and sweat" but not "blood and tears." James Reston.

New York Times. p50. D. 5, '54. Text of Stevenson's address at Democratic Committee dinner in New Orleans. A. E. Stevenson.

*New York Times. p E5. D. 26, '54. Communists find Asia ripe for subversion. H. R. Lieberman.

New York Times. p4. F. 4, '55. Faces show rigor of war in Malaya. Robert Alden.

New York Times. p6. F. 13, '55. Intrigue a threat to British Malaya.

New York Times. p E3. F. 27, '55. SEATO allies ask: How firm is U.S. commitment? Tillman Durdin.

*New York Times. p E2. Mr. 6, '55. Victory for Hatoyama.

New York Times. p E4. Mr. 6, '55. Aid-for-Asia program now up for decision. D. A. Schmidt.

New York Times. p E4. Mr. 6, '55. Dulles on tour learns southeast Asian problems. Robert Alden.

New York Times. p 10. Mr. 17, '55. Manila practices democratic rule. Robert Alden.

*New York Times. p28. Ap. 4, '55. Foreign affairs: South Korea's future is obscure. C. L. Sulzberger.

New York Times. p E6. Ap. 10, '55. Japan's politics puts a strain on U.S. ties. Robert Trumbull.

*New York Times. p4. Ap. 12, '55. U.S. policy on Quemoy, Matsu, and Formosa. A. E. Stevenson.

New York Times. p E5. Ap. 17, '55. Aid plan for 'arc of Asia' timed for Bandung parley. D. A. Schmidt.

New York Times. p E5. Ap. 24, '55. U.S. finds support among Afro-Asians. Tillman Durdin.

New York Times. p E4. My. 1, '55. Afro-Asians find it difficult to agree. Tillman Durdin.

*New York Times. p E4. My. 8, '55. U.S. now reappraising its policies toward free Asia. D. A. Schmidt.

New York Times. p E4. My. 15, '55. Asian nations balk at regional economic cooperation. A. M. Rosenthal.

New York Times. p3. Je. 2, '55. West's defense line in the Pacific. Foster Hailey.

New York Times. p E6. Je. 5, '55. Foreign aid set for another year. Allen Drury.

*New York Times. p8. Je. 7, '55. Indonesia backs neutralist aims. Robert Alden.

New York Times. p 10. Je. 9, '55. Tough army girds Korea truce line. Foster Hailey.

*New York Times. p4. Je. 10, '55. Five years harden troops of Korea. Foster Hailey.

New York Times. p E5. Je. 19, '55. Diem is gaining in south Vietnam. Tillman Durdin.

*New York Times. p E4. Jl. 17, '55. Divided Vietnam—comparison after one year. Tillman Durdin.

New York Times Magazine. p 12+. My. 23, '54. Malaya: jungle-bashing for C.T.'s. Vernon Bartlett.

New York Times Magazine. p7+. N. 21, '54. Saigon in the shadow of doom. Peggy Durdin.

New York Times Magazine. p9+. D. 12, '54. Portrait of a symbol named Nehru. Robert Trumbull.

New York Times Magazine. p9+. Ja. 2, '55. After seven years—report on India. Robert Trumbull.

New York Times Magazine. p 14+. Ja. 9, '55. Magsaysay fights a "social cancer." H. F. Wilkins.

*New York Times Magazine. p 13+. F. 6, '55. Model for U.S. propaganda. Peggy Durdin.

*New York Times Magazine. p 13+. F. 13, '55. Challenge we neglect in Asia. Barbara Ward.

*New York Times Magazine. p9+. Mr. 13, '55. It is not "down the drain." Barbara Ward.

*New York Times Magazine. p 13+. Mr. 13, '55. Analysis of communism in Indonesia. Peggy Durdin.

New York Times Magazine. p 12+. My. 15, '55. Reappraisal of the overseas Chinese. Peggy Durdin.

New York Times Magazine. p7+. Je. 5, '55. On trial—the white man in Asia. Peggy Durdin.

New York Times Magazine. p9+. Je. 19, '55. What the Asians expect of us. C. P. Romulo.

New Yorker. 31:39-78. Je. 11, '55. Four hours by rail from Jakarta. Christopher Rand.

New Yorker. 31:35-63. Je. 25, '55. Man in a mirror. Joseph Alsop.

Pacific Affairs. 28:3-25. Mr. '55. Indo-China since Geneva. B. B. Fall.

*pb: The Pocket Book Magazine. 1:66-80. N. '54. Those barbaric Americans. Emily Hahn.

*pb: The Pocket Book Magazine. 1:94-108. N. '54. Asians fear our foreign policy. Chester Bowles.

pb: The Pocket Book Magazine. 2:107-23. F. '55. Allies or satellites? Allan Nevins.

*Reader's Digest. 65:107-11. S. '54. Magsaysay: dynamic example for Asia. J. P. McEvoy.

*Reader's Digest. 65:136-46. N. '54. Pakistan: divided it stands. J. A. Michener.

*Reader's Digest. 65:57-66. D. '54. Thailand—jewel of Asia. J. A. Michener.

*Reader's Digest. 66:141-54. Mr. '55. Jimmy Yen and the people's crusade. J. P. McEvoy.

Reporter. 11:23-7. D. 16, '54. Malaya: the "emergency" in its seventh year. Han Suyin.

Reporter. 12:29-31. Ja. 13, '55. Indonesia: flotsam from the receding tide. Jean Lyon.

Reporter. 12:11-19. Ja. 27, '55. Enigma of Ho Chi Minh. Robert Shaplen.

Reporter. 12:19-20. Ja. 27, '55. Eyewitness report on Vietnam. Joseph Buttinger.

Reporter. 12:30-4. Ja. 27, '55. Men who really run Pakistan. Philip Deane.

Reporter. 12:14-17. Mr. 10, '55. Who are the Formosans? J. R. Dyer.

*Reporter. 12:19-20. Mr. 10, '55. An important link in the chain. T. R. Phillips.

*Reporter. 12:31-4. Ap. 7, '55. Job Harold Stassen leaves unfinished. H. A. Williams.

Reporter. 13:9-12. Jl. 14, '55. Strange neutrals of Panmunjom. H. J. Briner.

*Saturday Evening Post. 227:26-7+. Ap. 23, '55. Man on a rickety fence. Robert Sherrod.

Saturday Evening Post. 227:30+. Ap. 30, '55. Why Britain thinks we don't know what we're doing. E. O. Hauser.

Time. 64:19-22. Ag. 30, '54. Burma, the house on stilts.

Time. 64:32. N. 8, '54. Pakistan: the new dictatorship.

Time. 64:24-32. N. 22, '54. Indo-China, land of compulsory joy.

Time. 65:12-14. Ja. 24, '55. World trade: man with a puzzle.

*Time. 65:22-5. Ap. 4, '55. South Vietnam, the beleaguered man.

Time. 65:33. Ap. 11, '55. South Vietnam: night of despair.

*Time. 65:32-9. Ap. 18, '55. Man of the single truth.

Time. 65:26-8. My. 2, '55. Upset at Bandung.

*Time. 65:28. My. 2, '55. Member poses a question.

United States Department of State Bulletin. 30:593-7. Ap. 19, '54. America and the new India. J. D. Jernegan.

United States Department of State Bulletin. 31:3-6. Jl. 5, '54. United States and the uncommitted world. R. D. Murphy.

United States Department of State Bulletin. 31:799-803. N. 29, '54. Defense of Asia. R. D. Murphy.

*United States Department of State Bulletin. 32:126-31. Ja. 24, '55. The growing partnership among free nations. W. S. Robertson.
    Same abridged with title U.S. spokesman blasts red China. United States News & World Report. 38:90. Ja. 21, '55.

*United States Department of State Bulletin. 32:327-31. F. 28, '55. Our foreign policies in Asia. J. F. Dulles.

United States Department of State Bulletin. 32:521-6. Mr. 28, '55. Our bond with free Asia. R. D. Murphy.

United States Department of State Bulletin. 32:711-17. My. 2, '55. Recommendations for 1956 mutual security program. D. D. Eisenhower.

*United States Department of State Bulletin. 32:835-40. My. 23, '55. Our policies in Asia. R. D. Murphy.

*United States Department of State Bulletin. 32:854-6. My. 23, '55. Mutual security program—an investment in strength. J. F. Dulles.

*United States News & World Report. 37:24-8. S. 17, '54. Catastrophe in Asia. J. A. Van Fleet.

United States News & World Report. 38:19-22. F. 4, '55. Why U.S. is ready to fight for Formosa.

*United States News & World Report. 38:86-8. F. 4, '55. Can war now be outlawed from the world? Address at banquet sponsored by American Legion, January 26, 1955. Douglas MacArthur.

United States News & World Report. 38:71-3. My. 6, '55. Communists' ace diplomat usually gets what he wants.

United States News & World Report. 38:88-90. My. 20, '55. Reds' next aim in Asia; interview with Thailand's Premier, Field Marshal P. Pibulsonggram.

United States News & World Report. 38:63-4. My. 27, '55. Reds' newest weapon—Singapore students.

United States News & World Report. 38:134-43. My. 27, '55. A new plan to defeat communism. David Sarnoff.

United States News & World Report. 38:53-7. Je. 3, '55. Where dangers of war are greatest. H. F. Armstrong.

Vital Speeches of the Day. 21:1250-80. Je. 1, '55. Asian-African Conference. Soekarno and others.

15136